Wild Flowers

Chatto Nature Guides

British and European
Wild Flowers

Identified and illustrated with colour
photographs by

Dr. Dankwart Seidel

Photographed by

Wilhelm Eisenreich

Translated by Anthea Bell

English Edition edited by
David McClintock

Chatto & Windus · London

Published by
Chatto & Windus Ltd.
40 William IV Street
London WC2N 4DF

*

Clarke, Irwin & Co Ltd
Toronto

British Library Cataloguing in Publication Data

Seidel, Dankwart
  British and European wild flowers. —
    (Chatto nature guides).
  1. Flowers — Europe — Identification
  I. Title II. McClintock, David
  582'.13'094   QK281
  ISBN 0-7011-2323-0
  ISBN 0-7011-2324-9 Pbk

© BLV Verlagsgesellschaft mbH,
München, 1977
English Translation © Chatto & Windus
Ltd. 1978.

Printed in Italy

Introduction

We recommend that the reader look through this introduction since it will explain a number of technical terms which
occur in the book.

Anyone becoming interested in wild flowers, and wishing to
name them, finds himself confronted by a boundless variety
of species whose similarities and differences may encourage
him to know them better or, on the other hand, may prove
daunting.

Many of the excellent books on plant identification are rather
too detailed for someone in the early stages of studying wild
plants. In particular, matching a living specimen with the text,
or vice versa, often presents great difficulties. Here,
illustrations can be extremely valuable. If we want first and
foremost a representation which is as true to life as possible,
then photographs ought to be more effective than any
standardized drawing; but even photographs can never quite
replace a precise description.

So this book offers, in particular the beginner, an
introduction to the world of wild flowers, with pictures and
complimentary text. A first glance of this kind at some wild
plants and a gradual familiarity with botany, may well lead to
a wish to extend and deepen such knowledge, and to go on to
more advanced works.

We have to make certain compromises when we are trying to
make a survey such as this. The number of wild flowering
plants in Europe is estimated at about 16,000, naturalized, as
well as native species. Of these, about 2,500 are widespread;
this number is about the same as the total of Central
European species. The recognized British list is about three
quarters of this figure. Even to enumerate all the common
species of this area would overstep the confines of this book
by a long way. Therefore a selection had to be made, and in
this introductory guide trees and shrubs are omitted, as well as
grasses and sedges, which, though common, are mostly rather
daunting for a beginner.

The Book is about European and British wild flowers and we therefore include a very few plants not found in the British Isles but in Europe, because so many people visit Europe every year and so often they are on holiday, when they have time to look around them.

Although to cover such a huge subject in a relatively small book is very difficult, we include a little, quite advanced information in our descriptions of the flowers; descriptions of intricate adaptations for pollination and seed dispersal, for instance, must open the eyes and add to the interest of anyone with the least liking for natural history.

Essentially this guide covers herbaceous flowering plants, including one or two dwarf shrubs which are common in Central Europe, and characteristic of neighbouring areas. (Since there will be a separate guide to Alpine flowers, we have not dealt with purely Alpine plants here, though we do refer to the appearance in Alpine regions of those dealt with in this book; this will be found where references are made to the altitude a plant attains, or to the sort of soil it prefers.)

The plants described are to be found in such common habitats as deciduous, coniferous and mixed woods, meadows, heaths, cultivated ground, (fields, gardens, etc.), damp or rocky places and ruderal habitats. (Ruderal plants are those which occur in habitats influenced by Man, especially where the soil is rich in nitrogen, e.g. by pathsides, on rubbish dumps or by railways).

The plants in this book are generally systematically arranged. Where nomenclature is concerned, many species have a variety of popular names, but the most common is used here. This may also help the beginner to get used to employing from the start, the correct scientific name which avoids ambiguity.

The scientific name, in binomial nomenclature (introduced by Linnaeus), consists of two parts — the generic name and the specific epithet. Where the same species has been given several names, the principle of priority is applied: i.e. only the oldest validly published name is used. Example: *Ranunculus bulbosus*: — generic name — *Ranunculus* (Buttercup), and specific epithet — *bulbosus* (bulbous). One or more species form a genus, one or more genera a family.

The descriptions accompanying the photographs include the English and the scientific names, the family to which the plant belongs (also given in English and scientific terminology), a brief description of the species with its most important

distinguishing features, information about its habitat and distribution, as well as any remarkable or characteristic facts of general biology and floral ecology. In many cases information about the practical uses of the plant follows.
A brief survey of the botanical terms used in the text may help.

Structure of flowering plants

The diagram illustrates the structure of a typical flowering plant.

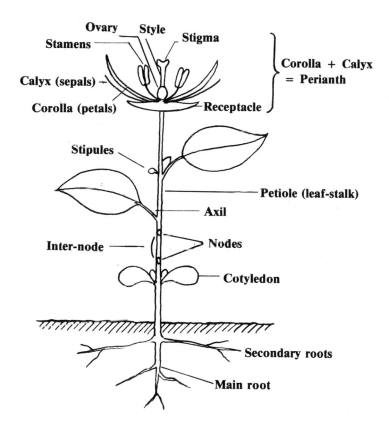

Root: The primary root together with secondary roots of various kinds form the root system. The root is characterised by its lack of leaves. Underground stems (rhizomes), bear at least pale, scale-like leaves, or the scars of such scales. Besides their functions of absorbing water and mineral salts, and anchoring the plant in the soil, the roots of many plants also store food. This generally results in the formation of fattened roots such as tap roots (e.g. dandelion), roots of the carrot type (wild carrot), or tuberous bulbs in roots (e.g. Lesser Celandine). In many species shoots can be formed from the roots for vegetative propagation (Toadflax Bindweed).

Stem: The main stem of a plant is usually divided into nodes and inter-nodes. The leaves are arranged in a distinctive way at each node. Branches grow from the axillary buds, which are known as Bract leaves.

If the main stem dominates the branches, we have what is called a monopodial system; if the side branches over-top the main stem, we call it sympodial. Similar relationships and terms occur with the forms of inflorescences (see diagram — p.   ); for instance, two opposite lateral buds growing taller than the central bud form a dichasium (the Pink Family).

Some specialized formations of the stem are thorns, tendrils and twining petioles, stems compressed into rosettes or bulbs, rhizomes (e.g. couch-grass), runners (above ground, e.g. the Strawberry) and tubers (Potato).

Leaf: First to develop are the *cotyledons* which have been laid down in the seed; in the dicotyledons (Magnoliatae) two usually develop, in the conocotyledons (Liliatae) one. They are rich in nourishment and provide for the embryo before it can manufacture its own organic matter, especially carbohydrate, by means of photosynthesis. Photosynthesis occurs in the mature, green leaves. Often *juvenile leaves* of even simpler structure are formed between the cotyledons and the mature leaves, which, however, in many cases, strongly resemble the latter.

Bracts are usually small, leaf-like structures at the base of flowers or flower stalks, above the normal leaves. They often form part of the perianth (e.g. in Buttercups). In the Diasy and Teasel Families the whole flower-head is enclosed in a group of smaller involucral bracts, umbellifers have both bracts (under the main umbels) and bracteoles (under the lesser umbels). In many cases the bracts are strikingly coloured, and take over the function of attracting pollinators which is usually done by the corolla; a poinsettia is an example.

In some families (among them the Rose, the Peaflower, and the Violet Families) *stipules* appear as growths at the base of the leaf. Generally they are simple and not striking in their structure, although in some cases they can look like normal leaves, making it difficult to differentiate between the two.

Leaves can vary a great deal in shape. The technical terms used to describe them in the book should make it easy to get an idea of their appearance. An ordinary leaf consists of a blade, a stalk or petiole, and a base. In simple leaves the blade is undivided, though some degree of indentation may be found. Composite leaves have several individual, separate leaflets or pinnae (e.g. pinnate leaves). These are generally arranged in pairs along the central axis corresponding to the midrib of a simple leaf. If the pinnate leaves themselves are further divided we have a bi- or tri-pinnate form.

Finally the margins of the leaf are often a help in identification.

Flower: The following structures, which have evolved from leaves, appear along the axis of the flower. From below to above they are: the *calyx, corolla* (together forming the perianth), stamens and styles, the latter attached to the ovary. While the calyx is generally developed from bracts, the corolla may be traceable to sterile stamens which have evolved leaf-like characteristics.

If there is no clayx the perianth is called a simple perianth. When there is a calyx (usually green) and a corolla of a different colour it is called a double perianth. When the calyx and corolla are similar in size and colour, the perianth is often called a *perigon* (e.g. wood anemone).

The main function of the corolla is to attract pollinators, usually visually. This is achieved by bright colour and special markings, usually of a different colour called honey guides. Many flowers which appear uncoloured to the human eye reflect ultra-violet light which can be perceived by numerous insects. In the way flowers are adapted to attract pollinators there is a tendency to modify originally radiate flowers, with separate petals, (i.e. not fused together), to monosymmetrical flowers with a fused corolla.

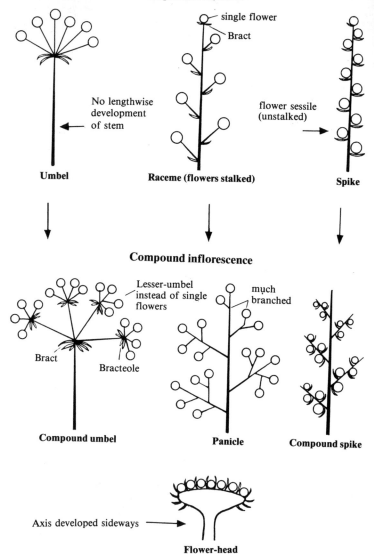

Simple inflorescence

single flower

Bract

No lengthwise development of stem

flower sessile (unstalked)

Umbel

Raceme (flowers stalked)

Spike

Compound inflorescence

Lesser-umbel instead of single flowers

much branched

Bract

Bracteole

Compound umbel

Panicle

Compound spike

Axis developed sideways →

Flower-head

The stamens, taken as a whole, are described as the *androecium,* and the stigmas, styles and ovaries as the *gynoecium.* In the latter it is important to note whether the carpels (the portions of the ovary) are separate from one another, (the mark of an earlier type of flower, e.g. the Buttercup Family), or are fused, (a more advanced feature) (e.g. umbellifers flowers, Labiates and Lillies). If the stamens and main part of the corolla are situated below the ovary, it is described as superior, and as inferior if they are above it.

The inflorescence is very important in the identification of plants. A single flower only forms in comparatively rare cases. The accompanying diagram shows some of the most common types.

Fruit: We can distinguish between dehiscent, indehiscent or multiple fruits.

Dehiscent fruits open when ripe to release their seeds. Each follicle or pod develops from a single carpel. When ripe, however, a follicle opens only at its front joint, a pod at both front and back. Examples: follicle — Marsh Marigold; pod-members of the Peaflower family.

Two carpels form a capsule, with a false septum between them. We can distinguish between capsules according to their methods of opening: those with pores (Poppy), "lidded" capsules, (Henbane) and those that split open (St. John's-wort, Autumn Crocus).

Indehiscent fruits remain closed when ripe and are dispersed together with the seeds they contain. According to the nature of the outer part of the fruit, we distinguish between berries (fleshy outer covering, one or more seeds inside), nuts (hard, woody, thick-walled, with generally only one seed) and stone fruits (the fruit containing a kernel inside a hard covering which in its turn has a fleshy covering).

Nuts have several special forms: e.g. achenes of the *Compositae* (Daisy Family). Here the fruit and the shell are fused. In many plants the hairy calyx (*pappus*) persists, to serve as an organ of flight. There are nuts where the individual carpels separate when the fruit is ripe (e.g. umbelliferous), and form single-seeded nuts.

Multiple Fruits develop from flowers where the carpels have not fused into any ovary. Examples: Strawberry (nutlets), Rasberry, Blackberry (stones) and Apple.

Types of flowering plants

The descriptions in this book attempt to take into account the changing relationship between the plant described and ecological factors, as well as describing them from the morphological point of view. The influence of factors such as light, water, temperature and soil involves many interesting considerations, which also affect the colonisation by plants of given habitats, and their geographical distribution.

Furthermore, the assignment of a plant to a certain life form is revealing when we consider its ecological adaptation. So, to conclude, here is briefly the division of plants according to their life forms.

Therophytes are essentially annuals, whose entire life cycle, from germination to the ripening of the seed, occurs within one year. They survive the unfavourable season as seeds, (e.g. Shepherds Purse).

Water plants, or *hydrophytes,* are particularly suited to the ecological factor of water.

Plants which survive unfavourable conditions (e.g. winter, periods of drought) by the formation of underground organs (bulbs, tubers, rhizomes) are called *geophytes* (Autumn Crocus, Solomon's Seal).

Hemicryptophytes bear their dormant buds at soil level. This group includes especially rosette and tufted plants (Daisy, Yarrow).

Chamaephytes are plants with buds up to 25 cm above the ground. They include many perennials, cushion-type plants and dwarf shrubs (Heather, Thyme, Rock Rose).

The larger woody plants are called *phanerophytes.* Their buds are freely exposed to the air during winter.

Of all the plant types, the *geophytes* (or *cryptophytes*) are the most sensitive to frost and low temperatures, and the *phanerophytes* are the most resistant. Among *chamaephytes* are typical plants of tundra and high mountains (above the tree line).

Wild Flowers

Marsh Marigold *Caltha palustria*

Buttercup family *Ranunculaceae*

Characters: 15-30 cm; flowers March-June, fleshy perennial with perianth of 5 bright yellow segments; diameter of flower 15-45 mm. Fruit: follicles containing many seeds, each formed of one carpel opening at the front joint. Stem with alternate, heart-shaped to circular, toothed, hairless leaves.—**Habitat:** marshy meadows, moors, streams, ditches, springs; damp and low-lying woods.—**Distribution:** circumpolar: North America — North and Central Europe — North Asia. Widely distributed all over the British Isles. The flowers of Marsh Marigold are pollinated by insects attracted partly by the bright yellow of the perianth, partly by special honey guides. These act as a kind of signpost to the nectar, and usually consist of particular lines and flecks of colour. The guides of the Marsh Marigold are perceptible only by insects with eyes sensitive to ultra-violet light; the flowers appear a uniform yellow to the human eye.

Wood Anemone *Anemone nemorosa*

Buttercup family *Ranunculaceae*

Characters: 15-20 cm; flowers March-April. Perennial, with usually a solitary flower; flower white, its 6-8 perianth segments often tinged with pink. Stamens numerous, yellow. Fruits deflexed; carpels hairy. The stem leaves are palmately divided; the basal leaves irregularly serrate or divided.—**Habitat:** deciduous and coniferous woods, copses, mountain pastures; up to 1900 m.—**Distribution:** Europe and Asia, but mainly in deciduous woods in West and Central Europe. Widely distributed all over the British Isles. Wood Anemone is one of the earliest spring flowers. It thus makes use of the relatively favourable conditions of good light before the emergence of the leaves on the trees; later on, the light in, e.g. beech woods, is unfavourable. Thus its entire life cycle occurs in spring. The flowers are pollinated by insects, but as a source of pollen belong to a very primitive type (cf. Common Poppy, *Papaver rhoeas*). The small nut fruit bears an appendage (elaiosom), which contains attractive, nutritional matter eaten readily by ants, who thus effectively disperse them.

Creeping Buttercup   *Ranunculus repens*

Buttercup family   *Ranunculaceae*   (Picture, top left)

Characters: 10-50 cm; flowers May-September. In contrast to the Bulbous Buttercup, the sepals are erect and appressed. The beak of the fruit is short and straight. The basal leaves have three lobes, the central with a clearly distinct stalk, all lobes trifid, toothed. A distinctive feature is the rooting runners.—**Habitat:** Favours damp parts of meadows, low-lying woods, gardens; by roadsides, ditches and Banks. Up to 2400 m in mountainous regions.—**Distribution:** world-wide in temperate climates. Common all over the British Isles. The runners enable it to colonize a new habitat quickly (a pioneering plant).

Bulbous Buttercup   *Ranunculus bulbosus*

Buttercup family   *Ranunculaceae*   (Picture, top right)

Characters: 10-50 cm; flowers April-May. Bulbous thickening at the base of the stem (hence the name), very hairy above. Flowers bright yellow, sepals deflexed. Fruits small, 2-4 mm, with curved beak. Leaves 3-lobed.—**Habitat:** relatively dry places — poor chalky grassland, meadows, pastures, fields, pathsides. Up to about 900 m.—**Distribution:** throughout Europe, especially in the West and North Mediterranean. Common all over the British Isles. Bulbous Buttercup likes warmth; it is somewhat poisonous.

Meadow Buttercup   *Ranunculus acris*

Buttercup family   *Ranunculaceae*

Characters: 30-100 cm; flowers April-October. This species differs from Bulbous Buttercup in its appressed, erect sepals, and the lack of a bulbous swelling at the base of the stem; and from Creeping Buttercup in its smooth, unbranched stem as well as the lack of runners. Flowers bright yellow, 10-25 mm. Stems almost appressed, hairy. Basal leaves long stalked with 5 to 7 lobes; stem leaves deeply toothed with 3 to 5 lobes.—**Habitat:** up to 2400 m in meadows, pastures, by roadsides, in copses.—**Distribution:** throughout Europe as far as Portugal and Turkey. Common all over the British Isles. Meadow Buttercup is typical of May meadows (cf. p. 66). It is poisonous, when fresh, but harmless in hay.

Lesser Celandine   *Ranunculus ficaria*
Buttercup family   *Ranunculaceae*

Characters: 5-20 cm; flowers March-May. 8-12 bright yellow petals (15-40 mm), usually 3 sepals. Leaves undivided, kidney-shaped to roundish heart-shaped, glossy; stem ascending. Plant mat-forming; perennial.—**Habitat:** low-lying woods, mixed deciduous woods, gardens, damp areas of parks; ditches. Up to 1100 m.—**Distribution:** throughout Europe, most common in the West, but reaching into Asia. Common throughout the British Isles. This species likes warmth, damp and shade or half-shade. Flies and bees pollinate it and ants disperse its seeds. As well as its sexual reproduction, it has an interesting a-sexual (vegetative), method: globular structures called bulbils sometimes grow in the axils of the upper leaves; rich with food, after a while they drop from the plant, take root and grow into new plants. In addition tuberous roots form at the base of the stem. The plant is poisonous.

Hepatica   *Hepatica nobilis*
Buttercup family   *Ranunculaceae*

Characters: 8-15 cm; flowers March-April. Flowers violet-blue, occasionally pink or white, long-stalked, 15-30 mm in diameter, of 6 to 9 binate segments. Sepals 3, ovoid, green. Leaves long-stalked, 3-lobed, appering after the flowers; often purple beneath. Stem hairy.—**Habitat:** open woods (beech and oak), copses; especially on chalk. Up to 1500 m.—**Distribution:** very disjunct (cf. p.26) in deciduous woods of the northern hemisphere: East Asia, Europe and North America (various geographical races). In Britian only in gardens. Hepatica is one of the earliest spring flowers. It is pollinated by insects; the seeds with their appendage (elaisom) contain nutrients attractive to ants, which thus disperse them. This particular form of dispersal is termed myrmecochory.

Corn Poppy   *Papaver rhoeas*
Poppy family   *Papaveraceae*

Characters: 20-80 cm; flowers May-August. One of the most familiar plants. Scarlet flowers with petals 2-4 cm long (generally with a black mark at the base). Its most important distinguishing feature is its fruit — a globose egg-shaped capsule of several fused carpels from which the seeds are scattered; less than twice as long as it is wide, and rounded at the base. 8-18 stigmatic rays. Flower stalk, leaves and stem, usually with stiffly spreading hairs. Leaves pinnately divided with narrow, coarsely toothed lobes.—**Habitat:** arable land (especially cornfields), waste ground, rubbish dumps, railway embankments. Up to 1000 m.—**Distribution:** Europe and Asia, but introduced all over the world. Still locally found in England and Scotland, scarce in the North West. Until quite recently the poppy family was placed directly next to the crucifers. However, in the light of new biochemical knowledge it is now put beside the buttercups, on account of its isochinolin-alkaloid content. This property is put to practical use in the extraction of opium from the opium poppy (*Papaver somniferum*). Common Poppy used to be considered an important healing herb. Its petals were also used to make red dye. However, it is not only one of our oldest agricultural weeds, dating back to the Neolithic era, but it shows very primitive characteristics from the point of view of floral ecology: it is one of the so-called "pollen flowers" which produce no nectar, but a great deal of pollen. Pollen, rich in protein, fat, carbohydrates and vitamins, attracted and provided food for primitive insects with biting jaws. In the history of evolution the development of nectar, and the simultaneous development of sucking jaws in insects such as butterflies, did not occur until much later. Finally, we should mention the interesting method of seed dispersal, seeds being scattered by the wind on a kind of "censer" principle.

Greater Celandine   *Chelidonium majus*
Poppy family   *Papaveraceae*

Characters:30-70 cm; flowers May-September. A typical perennial, ruderal plant, with golden, yellow flowers about 20 mm in diameter, in terminal umbels pf 2-6. 4 obovoid petals. Sepals yellowish, hairy. Stamens numerous. Fruit long (up to 5 cm), smooth; seeds black with white appendages (elaiosome). Leaves pinnate with irregular doubly crenate lobes, bluish-green beneath. The whole plant contains an orange-yellow latex.—**Habitat:**among other weeds, paths, walls, fences, copses, the borders of woods, hedges, wild park-land; found up to about 900 m.—**Distribution:** almost throughout Europe. Frequent in England and Wales, occasional elsewhere. Greater Celandine is a plant of great antiquity, indicating sites of human settlement and agriculture. It also indicates the presence of nitrogen in the soil. It is pollinated by insects, and the seeds dispersed by ants, who use the elaisome as a source of nourishment. The poisonous latex was once used as a cure for corns and warts, and the plant cultivated in certain areas for this purpose.

Nettle   *Urtica dioica*
Nettle family   *Urticaceae*

Characters: 30-125 cm; flowers June-October. Male and female flowers on different plants. Flower spikes longer than the leaf-stalks. Leaves coarsely toothed, long and pointed; stipules free. Stem erect with stinging, bristly hairs.—**Habitat:** a typical ruderal plant, found near human settlement, beside paths, on waste ground, but also in woods. Prefers damp, nitrogenous soil of which it is an indicator. Can occasionally be found as high as 2400 m.—**Distribution:** originally Northern and Central Europe and Asia, now worldwide. Common all over the British Isles. When touched, the stinging hairs penetrate the skin (like a syringe) and inject a liquid consisting of sodium formate, acetylcholine and histamine, which causes a burning sensation. A special feature of the Nettle is its method of pollination, the taut stamens springing back when the flowers have matured scattering their pollen.

Silverweed   *Potentilla anserina*
Rose family   *Rosaceae*

Characters: 10-50 cm; flowers May-August. Perennial with long, reddish runners and non-flowering shoots. Flowers solitary, yellow, 18-25 mm, on long stalks. Petals twice as long as the calyx. Leaves up to 25 cm long, irregularly pinnate, with 10-20 serrate leaflets covered with silky hairs, green above, silvery white beneath.—**Habitat:** open grassy places, goose-ground (hence anserina), rubbish dumps, pathsides, roadsides, ditches, banks. Up to 900 m.—**Distribution:** throughout most of Europe, and into West Asia; worldwide in very temperate zones. Common throughout the British Isles. Silverweed is an indicator of base rich, damp soil. It likes warmth and can tolerate relatively high concentrations of salt. Earlier, it was used medicinally.

Creeping Cinquefoil   *Potentilla reptans*
Rose family   *Rosaceae*

Characters: 30-90 cm; flowers May-August. A distinctive feature is the long, runner-like stem, taking root at the nodes (hence *reptans*). Leaves long-stalked, with 5-7 coaxial, serrate leaflets. Flowers solitary, yellow, 5 petalled, 8-12 mm long, on stalks from the leaf axils.—**Habitat:** hedges, meadows, fields, paths, ditches, banks; grows only up to 900 m.—**Distribution:** throughout Europe; now world-wide in temperate climates. Common throughout the British Isles. The runners make it an invasive plant which can quickly colonize empty ground. The flowers are pollinated by insects, and the fruits dispersed by mammals and ants. It once had a certain importance as a medicinal herb.

Wild Strawberry   *Fragaria vesca*

Rose family   *Rosaceae*

Characters: 5-25 cm; flowers April-June. Perennial with long runners rooting at the nodes and acting as a means of vegetative propagation; young plants usually formed at the ends. Flowers white, 15 mm, on leafless, hairy stalks. Leaves trifoliate, silky hair beneath and sparsely above. Fruit: consisting of numerous nutlets embedded in the swollen receptacle. Sepals spreading or reflexed.—**Habitat:** clearings in woods, felled woodland, woodland paths, copses, hedges; mostly among woodland plants where the ecological balance has been disturbed to some degree. In the Alps, up to 2200 m.—**Distribution:** rather like the Hepatica, (p.18) this plant has a somewhat disjunct distribution occurring in Europe, Asia and North America between which it seems impossible for it to spread in present circumstances. It occurs all over the British Isles. It likes sun or partial shade, is pollinated by insects, and the sweet-flavoured, juicy "berries" are dispersed by animals (and by man).

Lady's Mantle   *Alchemilla vulgaris*

Rose family   *Rosaceae*

Characters: 10-50 cm; flowers May-September. The small, greenish-yellow flowers are in cymes on long stalks; there are no petals, but 4 sepals; 4 stamens. Basal leaves roundish and long-stalked serrate, with 7-13 lobes. Plant with scattered hairs.—**Habitat:** meadows, pastures, near streams, the edges of woods and copses; also among scree.—**Distribution:** most of Europe and Asia. Frequent in N.W. Britian, rare elsewhere. Lady's Mantle is a good example of the phenomenon of guttation: after a damp, warm night large drops can be seen on the margins of the leaves. They are often thought, mistakenly, to be dewdrops. In fact this fluid has been expressed from so-called water stomate, minute openings on the leaf surface.

Great Burnet   *Sanguisorba officinalis*

Rose family   *Rosaceae*

Characters: 25-120 cm; flowers June-September. Flowers hermaphrodite, dark red, in dense, longish heads; stamens 4, with yellow anthers, style 1. Leaves pinnate, bluish green beneath; 7-13 leaflets (2-4 cm) with more than 12 teeth on each side.—**Habitat:** damp meadows, marshy ground, also pathsides. Up to a height of 1200 m.—**Distribution:** circumpolar; All Europe except for Iceland. Locally frequent in N. and Central England and in S. Wales, scarce elsewhere. Great Burnet — once used medicinally — is particularly interesting from the point of view of ecology. In this genus we can see a transition from pollination by insects (as in the great majority of members of the Rose family) to secondary pollination by wind. The hermaphrodite flowers of this species, with their 4 stamens, rough stigmas and nectaries are still clearly designed for pollination by insects. But wind-pollinated species of the genus no longer form nectar and have stigmas with a large, feathery surface, as well as numerous stamens.

Agrimony   *Agrimonia eupatoria*

Rose family   *Rosaceae*

Characters: 30-50 (100) cm; flowers June-September. Perennial with flowers in a long raceme. Petals yellow, ovate. Receptacle obconic, dense with spreading hairs, and 10 deep furrows; outer bristles erect or spreading, the inner curved inwards. Soon after flowering, the receptacle droops. Fruit about 6 mm long, obconical, hairy, with small, hooked bushes above (dispersal by sticking to animals etc.) Leaves pinnate, grey haired beneath. Stipules leaf like. Stem more or less round, coarse haired, with short glandular hairs above.—**Habitat:** meadows, poor grassland, heaths, pathsides, hedges, copses, edges of woods; especially on lime and clay. Up to more than 1000 m.—**Distribution:** Europe and Asia, with a slight preference for coastal areas. Common in South and Central England, rare in Scotland, occasional elsewhere. Agrimony likes warmth and partial shade. As a rule pollination is by insects, who take the pollen, which is produced in large quantities, for food.

Water Avens *Geum rivale*
Rose family *Rosaceae*

Characters: 20-60 cm: flowers April-August. Flowers nodding. Petals pink outside, yellow inside. Inner Calyx purple. Stamens over 10, style in two parts. Lower leaves long-stalked, pinnate, with large terminal leaflet, the upper simple or lobed; stipules small. Stem often several flowered; glandular hair above. Fruit terminated by the hooked, persistent style.—**Habitat:** water meadows, marshes, beside ditches and streams; low-lying woods, meadow land; up to 2000 m in the Alps.—**Distribution:** circumpolar; indeed almost all Europe. In the British Isles commonest in the North. Water Avens is frequently an indication of base-rich soil. It prefers a cool, humid climate and is pollinated by insects. The method of fruit dispersal is worth noting; the style remains on the fruit in the form of a hook and ensures adherence to animals. Another species, Herb Bennet, *Geum urbanum,* is also one of our common wild flowers. Like Water Avens, it has a hooked style. Herb Bennet can be distinguished from Water Avens quite easily; its flowers are erect, not drooping, and the petals are yellow; the sepals are finally reflexed. The basal leaves consist of 3-7 lobes or toothed pinnae, and here again the terminal leaflet is larger than the others. The stem leaves are usually trifid, but the upper leaves sometimes simple; the size of the stipules (almost as large as the pinnate leaflets) makes them a striking feature of the plant. This species prefers damp, shady places in woods, especially low-lying woodland areas, but occur occasionally in similar ruderal places.

Common Melilot   *Melilotus officinalis*
Pea family   *Fabaceae* (Papilionaceae)

Characters: 30-100 cm; flowers May-September. Flowers in racemes 4-10 cm long. The keel (the two fused front petals), shorter than the standard (the upper, enlarged petal) and the wings (the two side petals). Leaflet serrate with 6-13 pairs of veins. Fruit a pod, 3-5 mm long, hairless, finally brown.—**Habitat:** a typical ruderal plant; sunny, weedy areas, pathsides, rubbish dumps, near railways;: also on banks, in quarries, in grassy places; found up to 1000 m.—**Distribution:** Europe and Asia, especially in the west; world-wide in temperate areas. Occasional South England, scarce elsewhere. Common Melilot colonizes bare ground, and follows human settlements. It has many practical uses: for fodder and a source of nectar for bees, also to eat with herbal cheese, as a medicinal plant and to keep moths away. Its characteristic fragrance when it dries comes from coumarin, a glycosidal substance which also occurs in Woodruff (Galium odoratum), p.80.

White Melilot   *Melilotus alba*
Pea family   *Fabaceae* (Papilionaceae)

Characters: 30-120 cm; flowers May-August. An erect annual to biennial with white flowers in long, terminal racemes. Flowers 4-5 mm; standard (see above) longer than the wings. Pod 3-5 mm long, blunt, dark brown, net-veined, hairless. Leaves pinnate with 6-12 pairs of veins and a similar number of teeth, not always clearly marked; usually broadest in the middle. Stipules untoothed.—**Habitat:** a ruderal plant; roadsides, fields, railway banks, rubbish dumps, gravel pits. Prefers a sunny situation, warm in summer, on loamy soil, into foothills.—**Distribution:** almost all over Europe. Uncommon in the British Isles; last found in the South. White Melilot will conlonize waste ground, and is an agricultural weed. It has many medicinal and other uses. In some areas it is even cultivated as a source of nectar for bees and as green manure.

Black Medick   *Medicago lupulina*
Pea family   *Fabaceae* (Papilionaceae)

Characters: 10-60 cm; flowers April-September. Flowers 2-5 mm long, in almost globular heads of 10-50. Pod 2-mm curved, almost kidney-shaped, net-veined. Leaflets ovate, margins finally serrate, often with a small tooth at the apex. Stipules long pointed. Stem angular, prostrate or ascending.—**Habitat:** meadows, poor grassland, fields, banks, pathsides, railway embankments. Up to 1500 m.—**Distribution:** Europe and Asia, chiefly in the centre and south. Common in England and South Ireland, occasional elsewhere. Black Medick is another coloniser which will establish itself relatively quickly in open ground. It can be traced back as far as the Bronze Age in Southern Germany. It is pollinated by insects (bees), but self-pollination also occurs.

Bird's Foot Trefoil   *Lotus corniculatus*
Pea family   *Fabaceae* (Papilionaceae)»

Characters: 5-45 cm; flowers May-September. Flower in heads of 2-7, with three small bracts at the base. Flowers yellow, often tinged with red at the edges, up to 15 mm long. Keel (see p.32) bent at a right angle. Calyx teeth curved inwards in bud. Leaves ovate, wedge-shaped; stipules ovate, pointed, almost as large as the leaves; leaves glaucous beneath. Stem angular, ascending or prostrate.—**Habitat:** meadows, grassy places, fairly dry grass-land, copses, quarries, pathsides, among rocks. As high as 2300 m in the Alps.—**Distribution:** widespread in Europe and Asia, but mainly in the centre and west, and to the north of the Mediterranean. Common all over the British Isles. Bird's-foot Trefoil colonizes waste ground, and improves the soil. The plant is also of practical use as a source of nectar for bees and a good fodder plant.

Red Clover *Trifolium pratense*
Pea family *Fabaceae* (Papilionaceae)

Characters: 10-40 cm; flowers May-September. Flower-heads globular to ovoid, mostly in pairs, with two bracts; the bright pinkish-purple individual flowers are unstalked, 10-veined calyx, hairy on the outside. The long ovate trefoil leaves (1-3 cm) are generally blotched, the stipules sharply pointed.—**Habitat:** pastureland, fields, open woods, even water-meadows; at heights of up to 2300 m.—**Distribution:** world-wide, in cool or temperate parts. Common all over the British Isles. As a cultivated plant, with roots as deep as 2 m, Red Clover prefers a climate with mild winters. Over 50 cm annual rainfall is needed for its optimum development. Bumble bees pollinate the flowers, ants and herbivorous mammals disperse the seeds. Red Clover is of considerable importance agriculturally, as an indicator of base-soil, an improver of the soil itself (enriching it with nitrogen through bacterial symbiosis), and as a very valuable fodder plant.

White Clover *Trifolium repens*
Pea family *Fabaceae* (Papilioneceae)

Characters: 5-20 (50) cm; flowers May-October. Flower-heads of stalked white florets (turning light brown as they fade) with a 10-veined calyx. Stipules transparent, with green and purple veins, ending in an awn-like point. Stem creeping, rooting at the nodes.—**Habitat:** pasture land, parks, gardens, grassy places, pathsides; up to 2200 m in the mountains.—**Distribution;** the plant is found all over the temperate world and is common in the British Isles. An old associate of man, it is not only of great importance as a source of nectar for bees, but as fodder plant and for grazing. Its long, creeping stems enable it to colonize new areas quickly. It prefers well manured places, and is thus an indicator of nitrogen in the soil. As with Red Clover, dispersal of the seeds is by means of animals.

Crown Vetch   *Coronilla varia*
Pea family   *Fabaceae* (Papilionaceae)

Characters: 30-60 (120) cm; flowers May-September. The characteristic formation of the flowers of the Pea family, consisting of standard, keel and wing petals (see p.32), is here coloured as follows: standard, pink; keel (with a beaked tip) white, violet at the tip; wings white. The 8-20 flowers develop into four-angled fruits, 25-50 mm long, with a hooked beak and 3-6, 1-seeded joints. The stem, prostrate or ascending, is angular and hollow, the leaves with 4-12 pairs of leaflets.—**Habitat:** dry meadows, banks, edges of woods, bushy ground, quarries; chiefly on chalk; at heights of up to 1000 m.—**Distribution:** temperate areas of the continent especially in Central Europe and in the Balkans. It is rather rare in Britain. The plant is deep-rooting (about 1 m), slightly poisonous, likes open or partially shaded ground. The root shoots are noteworthy as a form of vegetative propagation: new ones from the inner layers sprout on the upper surface of the branch roots.

Tufted Vetch   *Vicia cracca*
Pea family   *Fabaceae* (Papilionaceae)

Characters: 20-150 cm; flowers June-August. Blue-violet flowers, 8-12 mm long, in dense racemes of 10-40. Leaves with narrow linear leaflets, up to 5 mm wide in 6-10 pairs. Stipules simple, arrow-shaped or pointed. Stems angular with extensive runners.—**Habitat:** banks, meadows, cornfields, copses on banks of streams; up to 1200 m.—**Distribution:** Europe and Asia. Frequent all over the British Isles. Tufted Vetch, climbing by tendrils, is a deep-rooted plant, and requires a relatively large amount of light to develop well. The flowers are pollinated by bees; dispersal of seeds is by the bursting of the pods or via the digestive processes of herbivores. It can be traced back to the Neolithic era.

Spring Pea   *Lathyrus vernus*

Pea family   *Fabaceae* (Papilioneceae)

Characters: 20-40 cm; flowers April-May. Perennial, hairless plant, with racemes of 3 to 8 flowers. Flowers 15-20 mm, purplish-pink at first, later blue to greenish-blue. Leaves with 4-6 long-pointed, broadly ovate leaflets, soft, glossy beneath, 3-7 cm long and 1-3 cm wide. Stem angular, unwinged. Fruit a dark brown pod, 4-6 cm long.—**Habitat:** woods and copses, especially in beech, oak and mixed coniferous woods; up to 1000 m.—**Distribution:** temperate continental areas of Europe, not wild in Britain, Portugal or the southern Balkans. A chalk-loving plant, of shade or partial shade, pollinated by bumble bees. It is one of the "second generation" of early-flowering plants. The beginner often has considerable difficulty in distinguishing between the closely related genera of *Vicia* (vetch) and *Lathyrus* (pea). It is a help to remove the petals and examine the staminal tube. (In the Pea family either all the 10 stamens, or 9 of them, are fused into a tube). If the staminal tube appears to be at right angles to the anthers (which are not fused) at the point of junction, then you have a species of Lathyrus; if the angle is oblique at the point of junction, you have a species of *Vicia*. It is easy enough to remember this by thinking of the right-angled shape of the letter L itself and the acute angle of the letter V (L for *Lathyrus,* V for *Vicia*). A few other species of *Lathyrus* should be mentioned here. Black Pea, *L. niger,* very rare in Britain, is fairly similar to the species described above, but its leaves have 8-12 leaflets, which are shorter and narrower, and turn black when dried (hence the name). Bitter Vetch *L. montanus,* quite frequent in Britain, can be identified by its narrowly winged stem, bluish-green leaflets and bright purple flowers, which turn blue as they go on. Narrow-leaved Everlasting Pea, *L. sylvestris* occasional in S. Britain, has a broadly winged stem and leaves with only two leaflets. Meadow Vetchling, *L. pratensis,* prefers damp meadow-land. This is the most common of British perennial, yellow-flowering species. Besides the tendrils on its leaves, which again consist of only one pair of leaflets, its relatively large sagittate or lanceoid stipules are a striking feature.

Wood Sorrel   *Oxalis acetosella*
Wood-sorrel family   *Oxalidaceae*

Characters: 5-15 cm; flowers April-May. A typical woodland plant, with solitary white or pale pink flowers; the petals with distinct violet veins. Basal leaves long-stalked with three pale-green obcordate leaflets. The plant has a rhizome (underground stem) which bears fleshy scales and the thickened scars of old ones.—**Habitat:** damp woods of mixed conifers, with plenty of humus in the soil, but also found in mixed oaks and beech woods. In the Alps up to a height of about 2000 m.—**Distribution:** circumpolar, particularly Northern Europe and Asia. The species is found throughout Europe and is frequent throughout the British Isles. This is a plant which definitely prefers shade, and has numerous peculiarities. As well as being pollinated by insects, it can pollinate itself even in bud; an explosive mechanism helps the dispersal of its seeds. Wood Sorrel used to be thought of very highly as a medicinal and useful herb; besides its medicinal uses, the leaves were eaten in salads. The whole plant is rich in oxalic acid and oxalates which, however, are poisonous taken in large quantities.

Herb Robert   *Geranaium robertianum*
Geranium family   *Geraniaceae*

Characters: 15-45 cm; flowers May-September. Flowers pink, 3-10 mm long, petals unnotched. Calyx glandular-hairy, only half the length of the petals, curved inwards at the top. Leaves pinnate, with 3 to 5 doubly pinnate, stalked leaflets. Stem (and leaves) glandular hairy, often reddish. The whole plant has an unpleasant smell.—**Habitat:** woods, ravines, shady walls, rocks, hedges, the edges of woods. Up to 1700 m.—**Distribution:** world-wide in temperate climates. Common all over the British Isles. The habitats show that this is a shade plant. The flowers are pollinated by insects or are self-pollinated; dispersal of seeds, as with other species of the Geranium family, is by an explosive mechanism.

Wood Crane's-Bill   *Geranium silvaticum*

Geranium family   *Geraniaceae*

Characters: 20-70 cm; flowers June-August. Flower stalks two flowered, erect as the fruit ripens (unlike Meadow Crane's-bill, *G. pratense*). Petals reddish purple, 12-18 mm long, hairy at the base. Leaves 7-lobed, deeply cut to over half way, irregularly toothed above. Plant hairy.—**Habitat:** meadows, woods, edges of copses, upland meadows, thick in hilly areas up to 2200 m.—**Distribution:** Central and Northern Europe and Asia. Quite frequent in N. England, Scotland. Wood Crane's-bill a plant of open or partially shaded ground, pollinated by insects. Its peculiar method of seed dispersal is described as a catapult mechanism; the inner parts of the carpels remain in the centre, forming a pillar, the outer walls of the ovary, each surrounding a seed below drop apart (only at the base, remaining fused with the central pillar at the tip) and catapult the seeds out of the fruit. This method of seed dispersal is typical of the entire *Geranium* family. About 20 species occur in Central Europe, and about twice that number can be found over the whole of Europe. Among the large-flowered species, along with Wood Crane's-bill and Meadow Crane's-bill, we find Bloody Crane's-bill *G. sanguineum,* not common in Britain, and Pyrenean Crane's-bill *G. pyrenaicum,* flowers 15-40 mm in diameter, local in the British Isles. Bloody Crane's-bill is easily recognized by its blood-red, solitary flowers — in other species, each stem bears two flowers. A typical feature of the Pyrenean Crane's-bill is its deeply notched, mauve petals; Meadow Crane's-bill is notable for its violet-blue, dark-veined petals, the filaments broadened below, and the drooping of its petals when it is over. Among small-flowered species, besides Herb Robert, (see p.42) the following are note-worthy: Round-leaved Crane's-bill, *G. rotundiofolium,* (scattered in the South of the British Isles), bearing soft glandular hairs, and Shining Cranes-bill, *G. lucidum,* (widespread on chalk and limestone) almost hairless — both with unnotched petals; Dove's-foot Crane's-bill, *G. molle,* (common in the British Isles) has long hairs on its stems and notched petals.

Touch-Me-Not   *Impatiens noli-tangere*
Balsam family   *Balsaminaceae*

Characters: 30-80 cm; flowers July-September. A distinctive annual with golden-yellow, pendulous flowers, 20-30 mm long, in racemes of 2 to 4 flowers. They have a curved spur and are monosymmetrical; the petals fused in pairs, with red-brown spots inside. The ovary is superior. Stem juicy, glossy often swollen at the nodes, much branched. Leaves alternate, stalked, ovate, coarsely toothed.—**Habitat:** damp woods, coniferous or deciduous, especially beech woods rich in humus; beside streams, woodland springs, in ravines and low-lying woods; in the Alps, up to 1300 m.—**Distribution:** Europe and Asia; over most of Europe. Rare in Britain. A shallow-rooting plant of good soil, generally pollinated by bumble bees (more rarely, self-pollination occurs). It is remarkable for the scattering method whereby it scatters its seeds, whence it gets its name of "Touch-me-not". The fleshy capsules, their tissues under great tension, spring open when touched and hurl the seeds for as far as 1 to 2 m.

Small Balsam   *Impatiens parviflora*
Balsam family   *Balsaminaceae*

Characters: 20-60 cm; flowers July-October. Annual, with small (8-10 mm) pale yellow erect flowers in racemes of 4-10. Flowers generally above the leaves. Spur straight and tapering Leaves tapered serrate, narrowed into the winged stalk.—**Habitat:** forms colonies in deciduous and coniferous woods, especially near their edges and by paths; gardens, parks, hedges, up to 700 m.—**Distribution:** this originated in North-Eastern and Central Asia. Since about 1837 it has escaped from botanical gardens and become naturalized almost throughout Europe, except in the most southern and western areas. It may be found throughout Britain. Small Balsam is a typical shade-loving plant, and indicates the presence of nitrogen in the soil. As with the preceding species, self-fertilization occurs as well as pollination by insects; the seeds are dispersed by the same explosive mechanism.

Wood Spurge   *Euphorbia amygdaloides*
Spurge family   *Euphorbiaceae*   (Picture top left)

Characters: 30-70 cm; flowers April-June. A perennial, with semi-woody biennial stems (most other native spurges are herbaceous), and an over-wintering basal rosette with long, obovate leaves tapered into the stalk, 4-7 cm long, from which the flowering shoots develop. Bracts fused in pairs to form a cupule, glands crescent-shaped. Fruit granulate.—**Habitat:** woods, copses, especially beech woods on chalk.—**Distribution:** all over Europe except for Northern Europe. Frequent in S. Britain.

Sun Spurge   *Euphorbia helioscopia*
Spurge family   *Euphorbiaceae*   (Picture top right)

Characters: 5-40 cm; flowers April-September. Annual, with generally 5-rayed umbels. Bracts yellowish green, ovate. Glands roundish ovate. Fruit smooth or at most very finely dotted. Stem erect, leaves increasing in size from bottom to top, alternate, tapering obovate, hairless; upper third slightly serrate.—**Habitat:** gardens, fields, waste ground; at heights of up to about 1000 m.—**Distribution:** throughout Europe, now found all over the world in temperate areas. It originated in the Mediterranean region. Frequent in most of the British Isles.

Cypress Spurge   *Euphorbia cyparissias*
Spurge family   *Euphorbiaceae*

Characters: 15-50 cm; flowers April-August. Leaves linear, narrow, entire, pale to bluish-green. Main inflorescence many rayed. Uppermost bracts not fused, yellow turning to red. Glands crescent-shaped, two horned, waxy yellow. Fruit rough.—**Habitat:** poor grassland, sheep pastures, dry slopes, rocky ground; prefers chalk; up to height of over 2300 m.—**Distribution:** almost throughout Europe, penetrating locally into Asia. Scattered in Britain, but rare. The white milky latex in the branched, non-articulated latex tubes, contains poisonous substances probably intended to protect the plant from being eaten; however, this may be true only of vertebrates, since the caterpillar of the spurge hawkmoth, for instance, feeds on the plant.

Hogweed   *Heracleum sphondylium*
Carrot family   *Apiaceae* (Umbellifeae)

Characters: 30-180 cm; flowering season June-October. Stout plant with angular, ridged, rough-haired stems. Umbels large, 5-15, rough-haired. Flowers white, the outer much enlarged, thus losing the normal multi-radiate symmetry of an umbellifer and making it appear mono-symmetric. This, however, produces a more striking visual effect, important for the attraction of insects. Bracts, none, bractieoles, anceolate. Leaves large (10-30 cm), pinnate, with ovate-lanceolate, stalked leaflets. Leaf-sheaths much enlarged. Fruit flat, broadly winged, with distinct oil-tubes, 7-11 mm long.—**Habitat:** meadows, ditches, banks, copses, edges of woods, pathsides.—**Distribution:** all over Europe penetrating into Asia. Common all over the British Isles. For its optimum development, Hogweed requires a humid climate. It is pollinated by flies and bees, and is a typical indicator of base-rich soil. It is a typical umbellifer. This family is now classified as one of the very diverse groups within the sub-class of *Rosidae*. The habit of these plants, which is similar in nearly all the species and genera, makes it easy to identify the family, but all the more difficult to tell the precise species. Umbellifers have the following features: their stems are distinctly divided into nodes and hollow internodes, leaves alternate, usually pinnate, but in any case divided; there is a characteristic leaf-sheath at the base of the petiole. Flowers five-petalled, radially symmetrical, and nearly always in compact umbels. The most common flower colour is white (occasionally yellow or pink). One of the most important identification features is the form of the fruit, which has ribs and grooves as well as resinous ducts (the oil tubes). The large number of medicinal and aromatic plants (for example caraway, anise, dill, fennel, parsley, carrot), found in this family may be attributed to its high content of essential oils.

Wild Carrot *Daucus carota*

Carrot family *Apiaceae* (Umbelliferae)   (Picture top left)

Characters: 50-80 cm; flowering May-August. Umbels (3-7 cm) slightly convex in flower; as the seeds ripen the rays curve inward to form a concave "bird's nest", central flower usually deep red, the others white, the outer often enlarged. Bracts 7-13 pinnate; bracteoles linear. Leaves 2-4-pinnate, hairy. Roots swollen.—**Habitat:** meadows, fields, roadsides, embankments, quarries; up to 1100 m.—**Distribution:** all over Europe; has spread all over the temperate world. Often abundant in most parts of the British Isles.

Cow Parsley *Anthriscus silvestris*

Carrot family   *Apiaceae* (Umbelliferae)   (Picture top right)

Character: 60-150 cm; flowering April-August. Flowers white, an umbel of 4 to 15 rays; outer florets slightly enlarged; bracts none, bracteoles 1-5. Leaves 2 to 3-pinnate. Stem hollow, ridged, hairy below, hairless above tip. Fruit 5-10 mm long, longer than its petiole, smooth, dark brown.—**Habitat:** pastures, hedges, copses, roadsides; in the shade of fruit trees; up to heights of 2400 m.—**Distribution:** Northern and Central Europe and Asia, but worst in the west. Often abundant in much of the British Isles. Cow Parsley is one of the most common umbellifers of Central Europe. As its flowers are relatively unspecialized, it is pollinated mainly by flies and beetles.

Ground Elder *Aegopodium podagraria*

Carrot family   *Apiaceae* (Umbelliferae)

Characters: 30-100 cm; flowers May-September. Vigorous, rhizomatous, perennial with angular, ridged, hollow stems and umbels 12-20-rayed, small white flowers; bracts and bracteoles, none. Leaves doubly ternate, fruits hairless.—**Habitat:** hedges, copses, gardens, cemeteries, banks, ravines in woods; in mountain areas up to about 1500 m.—**Distribution:** of mixed over almost all temperate Europe, including the British Isles.

Perforate St John's-Wort

Hypericum perforatum

St John's-wort family   *Hypericaceae*

Characters: 30-100 cm; flowers June-August. Erect perennial with translucent-dotted leaves and solid, hairless stem, with two raised lines lengthwise. Stem glandular above. Flowers relatively large, golden yellow, in clusters. Petals, generally asymmetrical, with black dots. Sepals entire, lanceolate-pointed, twice as long as the styles at flowering time. Fruit a capsule.—**Habitat:** dry slopes, poor grassland, roads, pathsides, edges of woods and scrub clearing in woods, meadows; at heights up to about 1000 m.—**Distribution:** all over Europe as far as Iceland; now all over the world in cool to temperate areas. Common in England and Wales, less so in Ireland, rare in the North of Scotland. The habitants show that this plant prefers full light or partial shade, and indicates poor soil. Perforate St John's-wort is also a colonizing plant. The flowers produce far more pollen than is needed for pollination. The excess is used by pollinating insects as food. As might be expected, self-pollination also occurs. The plant also contains aromatic oils, stored in special organs called "oil glands". These can be seen with the naked eye as translucent dots on the surfaces of the leaves. It is probably on account of this that Perforate St John's-wort was used as a magical and medicinal herb in the Middle Ages. It was employed to heal wounds, as a remedy for worms, and even to avert the danger of lightning. Several other species of St John'-wort occur not uncommonly: square-stalked St John's-wort, *H. terrapteuval,* and Imperforate St John's-wort, *M. maculatum,* both have squared stems: the latter without dots in the leaves. Pale St John's-wort, *U. montanum,* with hairy leaves, Hairy St John's-wort, *H. hisutum,* with almost woolly leaves, Slender St John's-wort, *H. pulchrum,* is indeed the slenderest.

Common Dog Violet   *Viola siviniance*
(riviniana)
Violet family   *Violaceae*

Characters: 5-30 cm; flowers April-June. No based rosette of leaves. Flowers pale violet, shading to white at the base, on stalks from the leaf axils. Spur 4-8 mm long, one to three times as long as the appendage of the sepal, white or yellowish. Stem ascending or erect, almost hairless; leaves long-stalked ovate, thickish. Stipules 5-10 mm narrow lanceolate, slightly toothed or fringed.—**Habitat:** woods, edges of woods, pathsides, banks; up to 1100 m.—**Distribution:** over nearly all Europe. Common all over the British Isles. Dog Violet is very variable. The flowers are pollinated by insects; an elastic mechanism disperses the seeds.

Wood Dog Violet   *Viola reichenbachiana*
Violet family   *Violaceae*

Characters: 10-30 cm; flowers April-June. Flowers less than 2 cm, reddish purple, petals not overlapping; spur violet, slender, usually curved downwards, 4-6 mm long. Lower leaves from the stem axils. Leaves heart-shaped, sparsely hairy; stipules linear-lanceolate, with comb-like fringes.—**Habitat:** deciduous woods (especially beech woods), coniferous woods, copses; up to heights of 1600 m.—**Distribution:** Wood Dog Violet is a typical Central European species, deciduous woods; it also appears in hilly areas of Southern Europe. Locally frequent in England and Wales, scarce in Ireland. If pollination by insects fails, self-pollination may take place. The seeds are distributed by ants.

Field Pansy   *Viola arvensis*
Violet family   *Violaceae*

Characters: 10-25 cm; flowers May-October. Unlike the true violets, the lateral petals of pansies are turned upwards, and are of different sizes and colours. Flowers 15-25 mm, yellowish to bluish yellow, upper petals usually violet; but odd yellow plants are quite common. Spur, at the most, half as long as the petals, and very little longer than the appendages of the sepals. Petals shorter than sepals. Pistil bent, with a capitate stigma. Leaves heart-shaped to lanceolate, longer than broad. Stipules very variable, generally pinnate, with a long, curved span. Stem branching, usually hairless.—**Habitat:** cultivated ground, roadsides, rubbish dumps, dunes; in mountain areas up to about 1000 m.—**Distribution:** all over most of Europe; spread all over the world in cool and temperate areas. And is common in the British Isles. Field Pansy is pollinated by insects, particularly bees, but self-pollination is fairly frequent. The capsules, which spring apart when open into three sections, have developed a special "squeezing" form of catapulting mechanism for seed dispersal. They are also distributed by ants. As with many other violets, Field Pansy was formerly used medicinally, and was valued in particular for the laxative and purgative qualities of its extracts. Wild Pansy, *Viola tricolor* differs from the species described above in having large flowers (to 25 mm), with petals longer than the sepals. It is much scarcer in the British Isles. Both species hybridize readily. There are two more Wild Pansies with bright yellow or violet flowers, the Seaside and the Mountain Pansies, *(Viola curtisii* and *V. lutea),* the former in dunes, the latter in upland pastures in Wales and in the North of the British Isles.

Common Rock-Rose

Helianthemum mummulerium

Rock-rose family   *Cistaceae*

Characters: 10-30 cm; flowers May-September. Perennial undershrub. Flowers yellow, variable in size (8-18 mm) in unilateral racemes. Leaves elliptical, green above, grey downy beneath. Stipules lanceolate, longer than the petiole. Like the flowers, the vegetative organs are extremely variable.—**Habitat:** dry, sunny places; heathland, pastures, edges of woods, dry slopes, rocky ground — especially on chalk, in the foothills.—**Distribution:** all over Europe except for Iceland and Norway. Widespread in the British Isles. Common Rock-Rose is one of the few members of the family to be found almost all over Europe. The area from which the family spread is the Mediterranean.

Common Rock-rose is a plant which needs light in order to germinate; a high intensity is necessary for its full development. Its stamens are irritable. As well as the plant described here, two other species of this group are found in the British Isles. Hoary Rock-rose, *canum* which has no stipules, and small leaves and flowers on the underside. White Rock-rose, *H. apenninum* with white-petalled flowers found in two locations in Somerset and Devon.

Shepherds Purse   *Capsella bursa-pastoris*

Cabbage family   *Brassicaceae* (Cruciferae)

Characters: 10-50 cm; flowers February-November. An extremely variable, usually annual, plant, with small white flowers in a terminal racemes. Petals are undivided, 2-3 mm long, twice as long as the sepals. The characteristic triangular, obcordate fruit 6-9 mm long, contains several seeds. The upper leaves generally undivided, with an arrow-shaped amplexicaul base (clasping the stem), the basal normally deeply pinnate.—**Habitat:** a typical ruderal plant; fields, gardens, rubbish dumps and path-sides; in the Alps up to over 2100 m.—**Distribution:** almost all over the world, cosmopolitan, common in the British Isles. Shepherd's Purse is a typical agricultural weed. Its self-pollination (as well as pollination by insects) and production of a large quantity of seeds are typical of pioneer plants of this nature, which are very often annual weeds. It is a great advantage to such to be able to colonize very quickly a habitat suitable for them for only a short time.

Field Pennycress   *Thiaspi arvense*

Cabbage family   *Brassicaceae* (Cruciferae)

Characters: 10-40 cm; flowers April-October. Annual, with white flowers in terminal racemes. Stem leaves amplexicaul, arrow-shaped at the base, hairless, angular; basal leaves ovate, stalked. Fruit a pod, flat, almost circular (up to 15 mm), broadly winged (see below):—**Habitat:** weedy areas, fields, cornfields, rubbish dumps; up to heights of 1300 m.—**Distribution:** All over Europe, to the Eastern Mediterranean, a large part of Asia; widely introduced. Frequent in South-east Britain; occasional elsewhere. Field Pennycress has been a typical agricultural weed since the Neolithic times. As with many annuals, self-pollination occurs as well as pollination by insects. The plant's method of seed dispersal is particularly interesting; it belongs to the so-called "rain catapulting" plants. The fruits are shaped like turbine blades, at the end of long stalks; the force of falling raindrops sets them into a catapulting motion which flings the seeds out.

Charlock *Sinapis arvensis*
Cabbage family *Brassicaceae* (Cruciferae)

Characters: 20-60 cm; flowers May-September. Annual, with yellow flowers (9-12 mm); sepals spreading. Fruit a pod (over three times as long as broad) with a straight, tapering beak, usually hairless. Upper leaves unstalked, more or less undivided; the lower stalked, deeply pinnately-lobed, with large terminal lobes. Stem rough-haired.—**Habitat:** rubbish dumps, roadsides, fields, waste ground; up to 1000 m.—**Distribution:** world-wide, in temperate areas. Common in the British Isles. Charlock (also known as Wild Mustard) avoids acid conditions, and is thus an indicator of basic soil. Only poor quality mustard can be made from it (often used in blends!). The seeds of White Mustard, *Sinapis alba,* on the other hand, have a good oil content, and are used to make mustard. The oil from these plants can irritate the skin.

Wild Radish *Raphanus raphanistrum*
Cabbage family *Brassicaceae* (Cruciferae)

Characters: 20-60 cm; flowers May-September. A distinctive feature is the fruit; a long pod (2-10 cm × 15-50 mm), formed of bead-like sections which break up separately when ripe. Petals white with violet veins; more rarely pale yellow. Sepals erect (unlike those of the Charlock). Upper stem leaves undivided, lower with 1-4 narrow pinnate lobes on either side, with a large terminal lobe. The whole plant is rough-haired.—**Habitat:** with other cornfield weeds, on rubbish dumps, on cultivated land, in sandy soil; up to 1300 m.—**Distribution:** the species originated in the Mediterranean area, but has now spread all over the temperate world. It is frequent over most of the British Isles. Wild Radish has been a weed of agriculture since Neolithic times, especially in rye fields. It is one of the commonest weeds of arable land but has practical uses as a source of nectar for bees and as a salad plant. It is closely related to the Garden Radish, *R. sativus* whose pods are not beaded, many varieties of which are cultivated.

Lady's Smock   *Cardamine pratensis*
Cabbage family   *Brassicaceae* (Cruciferae)

Characters: 15-50 cm; flowers April-July. Perennial of meadows, petals white, but also often pink or mauve, in a close raceme. Petals about three times as long as the sepals; stamens yellow. Fruit a beaked pod. The pinnate leaves are also characteristic of this plant; the upper with lanceolate, the lower with ovate leaflet. The basal leaves are in rosettes with 3-11 leaflets, the terminal distinctly larger than the others. Stem hollow and round.—**Habitat:** damp meadows, marshland, low-lying woods, banks, in the Alps up to heights of over 1700 m.—**Distribution:** circumpolar. Very common in Northern and Central Europe and Asia, and the British Isles. Lady's Smock is part of the spring aspect of our meadows. The appearance of a plant community changing with the seasons is generally described as its aspect. If a plant community is to be fully understood, then we must consider it in all its aspects. The sequence of aspects of a meadow with false Oat grass *(Arrhenatherum elatius),* for instance, might be marked by the following plants from March to August: Lady's Smock, Daisy, Dandelion, Meadow Buttercup, Ox-Eye Daisy. Cow Parsley, Meadow Cranesbill and Hogweed. Lady's Smock is an indicator of base soil. The flowers are pollinated by insects; an ejaculating mechanism disperses the fruits.

Garlic Mustard   *Alliaria petiolata*
Cabbage family   *Brassicaceae* (Cruciferae)

Characters: 25-100 cm; flowers April-June. Erect, hairless plant; smelling of garlic when pressed, hence its name, the smell being especially marked in the roundish heart-shaped, toothed leaves. The terminal raceme bears white flowers 6 mm long, the petals twice as long as the sepals. Fruit, a 4-angled pod, 3.5-7 cm. long. Stem angular.—**Habitat:** walls, hedges, fences, neglected gardens and parks, edges of woods, weedy ground; up to 1000 m, not found in the Alps.—**Distribution:** chiefly in the Centre and West (in Europe and Asia). Frequent in English woods, occasionally in Southern Scotland.
Garlic Mustard was formerly used as a salad plant and a medicinal herb. In addition to pollination by insects, the plant can be self-pollinated.

Heather   *Calluna vulgaris*
Heath family   *Ericaceae*

Characters: 20—50 (100) cm; flowers July-October. Evergreen dwarf shrub with purplish-pink flowers, in dense, somewhat unilateral racemes, (up to 15 cm long); flowers on curved stalks, 4 mm. The calyx resembles, and is longer than the corolla with green bracts beneath. Stamens 8; the anthers have two long horns, and open by pores to the pollen. Fruit a capsule. Leaves in four, 1-3.5 mm long.—**Habitat:** heaths, poor pastures; open, dry woods (pine, oak); hoggy poor rocky round. Especially on poor acid soil; will grow at heights of over 2500 m.—**Distribution:** all over Europe, including the British Isles, except in the Balkans, into Siberia. Heather is a wind-pioneer resistant plant, degrading the soil, and requiring light to germinate. Its symbiosis with fungi *(mycorrhiza)* is particularly important. It has many practical uses, especially for northern people for fuel, brooms, and brushes, litter and thatch. It is also important to beekeepers as a rich source of nectar for heather honey.

Oxlip   *Primula elatior*
Primrose family   *Primulaceae*

Characters: 10-30 cm; flowers March-May. Corolla with lobes flat at the edges, sulphur yellow; dark yellow at the mouth of the tube. Very little if any scent. Calyx appressed to the corolla. Leaves 10-20 cm, puckered, with scattered, short hairs.—**Habitat:** deciduous woods, especially in damp, low-lying areas; copses, meadows, up to heights of 2400 m.—**Distribution:** almost all over Europe, especially in the west, centre and south. In Britain locally, abundant in a small area of East Anglia. Oxlips form the springtime aspect (see Lady's Smock, above) of meadows. A special phenomenon, heterostyly, ensures cross-pollination of the flowers by bees and bumble bees: the plants bear in roughly equal numbers flowers with short styles i.e. thrum, or long styles i.e. pin-uied. The stamens are correspondingly inserted either high or low. Darwin was able to show that the pollen from thrum plants had to be carried to a pin flower, while the pollen of a pin flower was best transferred to the stigma of a thrum flower; only this cross-pollination will produce an optimum set of fruit. Even the size of the pollen grains and the papillae of the stigma are distinguishable in the two forms.

Cowslip   *Primula veris*
Primrose family   *Primulaceae*

Characters: 10-30 cm; flowers April-May. Unlike the Oxlip, the outer lobes of the cowslip are not flat; the corolla is deep yellow, with 5 orange spots at the mouth of the tube (honey-guides). The flowers have a strong scent; calyx bell-shaped. Leaves 5-15 cm. fairly long, narrowing towards the winged stalk, hairy velvety, like the stems.—**Habitat:** meadows, open woods, edges of woods, copses; preferring poor chalk grassland; up to heights of 1700 m.—**Distribution:** abroad the same as the Oxlip, but, widespread in the British isles. Cowslips like light and warmth and exhibit the phenomenon of the heterostyly. In both species the seeds are dispersed by the wind, i.e. movement of the air scatters the seeds from the capsules at the top of the tall stems. The roots of the fragrant Cowslip were formerly used for medicinal purposes.

Bladder Campion   *Silene vulgaris*
Pink family   *Caryophyllaceae*

Characters: 10-60 cm; flowers May-September. Perennial with white flowers, and a distinctive inflated, pale, hairless, 20-veined calyx. Petals deeply cleft in two. Erect or ascending stems. Lanceolate-ovate, bluish green leaves.—**Habitat:** poor grassland, rocky or stony areas; edges of copses, railway embankments, pathsides; in low ground and onto hills.—**Distribution:** all over Europe; widely introduced. Frequent in the British Isles, most common in the south. Bladder Campion is a relatively undemanding plant which colonizes open ground. Pollination is chiefly by moths, but also bees. It used to be valued medicinally.

Red Campion   *Silene dioica*
Pink family   *Caryophyllaceae*

Characters: 30-80 cm; flowers April-September. A dense glandular-haired biennial to perennial, with dioecious (see below) red flowers, which open only during the day. Styles 5. Capsule globular, with 10 revolute teeth.—**Habitat:** (damp) meadows, deciduous woods, hedges, clearings; occuring in the Alps up to heights of 2400 m.—**Distribution:** Europe and Asia, most common in the centre and west, not in the southern Balkans or Asia Minor. Common in Britain, local in Ireland.

Red Campion has the characteristic features of flowers which are pollinated almost exclusively by butterflies and moths (in this case butterflies), and only rarely by bumble bees. The white flowers of the closely related White Campion, *M. album,* do not open until evening, and are sought out by moths, especially hawk-moths. The flowers are dioecious (i.e. the male and female flowers are on separate plants). This ensures cross-fertilization.

Ragged Robin *Lychnis flos-cuculi*

Pink family *Caryophyllaceae*

Characters: 30-90 cm; flowers May-August. Branched perennial, with flesh-pink to deep pink flowers, their petals 4, cleft to below the middle. Flowers about 3 cm in diameter. Calyx 10-veined, 6-10 mm long, usually reddish. Inflorescence loose, with dichasial branching (c.f. Greater Stitchwort, *Stellaria holostea,* see page 76). Stem leaves narrowly lanceolate, smooth based, spathulate, often ciliate, stalked. Stem appears hairy.—**Habitat:** pasture land, marshy places, water-meadows, damp copses, (to be met with at heights of 1400 m.).—**Distribution:** in humid areas, over Europe and Asia. (Humid areas are those where evaporation is less than rainfall). Frequent all over the British Isles. Ragged Robin is a typical indicator of worst ground which it reflects by its habitats. As with most members of the pink family, the flower is of a type where pollination is carried out mostly by butterflies, whose 2-4 cm long proboscis can reach the nectar at the base of the flower tube. The mutual adaptation of flower and pollinator in this case is obviously further developed than, for instance, in Common Poppy, *Papaver rhoeas* (p.20). The specific epithet seems inexplicable at first, but if one looks at several plants, one finds something like spittle on many of the stems in which the larva of the frog-hopper conceals itself. Its excretions, mingled with air, form a foamy lump which protects it from predatory enemies. Once upon a time this foamy substance was thought to be cuckoo-spit; hence the name.

Greater Stitchwort   *Stelleria holostea*
Pink family   *Caryophyllaceae*

Characters: 10-45 cm; flowers April-June. The white petals (10-15 mm long) are about twice as long as the unveined sepals, and are divided to halfway. Styles 3. Fruit a globular capsule, which opens into 6 sections. Leaf-like. Leaves sessile, ever-green. Stem 4-angled. The inflorescense of Greater Stitchwort is typical of the pink family: the main stem stops growing quite early, but pairs of side branches continue to grow which in their turn are taken over by further side branches. The resulting inflorescence is described as a dichasium.—**Habitat:** deciduous woods, copses, hedges.— **Distribution:** all over Europe, especially in west and centre to foothills of the mountains. Frequent in most of British Isles.

Bistort   *Polygonum bistorta*
Dock family   *Polygonaceae*

Characters: 30-80 cm; flowers May-June. Flowers 4-5 mm long, pink, in cylindrical dense spikes, 3-5 cm long. Basal leaves longish ovate, pointed, up to 15 cm long, narrowing towards the wavy-edged stem. Dark green above, bluish green beneath. Upper stem leaves sessile, with a heart-shaped base. Stem unbranched; rhizome thick, banal-shaped, snake-like.—**Habitat:** damp meadows, low-lying woods, banks up to 1800 m.—**Distribution:** Northern Europe, almost circumpolar — strangely enough, however, it is not native in Scandinavia. Most common in the North of England, occasional elsewhere in Britain, rare in Ireland. Bistort or Snakeweed is a very deep-rooted plant, and has a certain importance as a bee food and for fodder.

Common Sorrel   *Rumex acetosa*
Dock family   *Polygonaceae*

Characters: 30-100 cm; flowers May-June. Erect perennial, with an open bractless inflorescence; flowers pale pink. Outer perianth segments reflexed. A dioecious plant. Stem leaves pointed or arrow-shaped; root leaves long-stalked, longish ovate, 2-3 cm wide. The ochrea (a papery sheath enfolding a node, formed of fused stipules, and typical of the dock family) is toothed or torn.—**Habitat:** meadows, grassy places, open places in woods, banks; up to heights of 1600 m.—**Distribution:** circumpolar, mainly in Central and Northern Europe and Asia. Found all over the British Isles. Common Sorrel forms a characteristic of aspect (see above) of meadows from May to June. It indicates the presence of nitrogen in the soil. Its value for fodder is relatively small; it is of more importance as a medicinal herb and for human consumption, the leaves being used for salads. A close relative is Sheep's Sorrel, *Rumex acetosella,* which is found in dry grassland, heathland and other sandy places. In this species the outer perianth segments are erect, the inner, unlike those of the Common Sorrel, have no tubercles. Among other common species of the genus is Curled Dock, *R. crispus,* which is notable for the long lanceolate root leaves. Broad-leaved Dock, *R. obtusifolius,* has heart-shaped lower leaves and large, blunt upper leaves. These two also differ in the shape of the inner perianth segment. In the Curled Dock, they are entire, round to heart-shaped, in Broad-Leaved they have 2-5 teeth. Water Dock *R. hydrolapathum,* is found by standing water or rivers. Its inner perianth segments are also entire, but have tubercles. The longish-elliptical, pointed basal leaves, narrowed below, can reach a length of about 1m. Two other species are commonly found: Clustered Dock, *R. conglomeratus,* and Wood Dock, *R. sanguineus.* Both are notable for their longish, narrow inner perianth segments; in the former most of the inflorescence has bracts in the latter only the lower flowers.

Woodruff   *Galium odoratum*
Bedstraw family   *Rubiaceae*

Characters: 10-30 cm; flowers April-June. The plant has
creeping rhizomes, and relatively thin, 4-edged stems
(smooth, apart from a few hairs at the nodes). Leaves in
whorls of 6-9, over 5 mm broad. Flowers pure, white clusters,
the corolla with a distinct tube, 6-7 mm long, and 4 blunt
spread lobes. Fruit with hooked bristles.—**Habitat:** deciduous
woods, especially beech woods; up to 1400 m.—**Distribution:**
Woodruff, a typical plant is mixed deciduous woods, is one of
those Central European species which also occur in Southern
European mountain areas. It is to be seen all over the British
Isles. The following ecological features are remarkable;
Woodruff is a shade-loving plant, pollinated by bees and flies,
and is spread by its burry fruits. Its characteristic scent comes
from the coumarin it contains, but is not perceptible until the
plant is crushed or dried. The biosynthesis of this important,
fragrant and spicy substance derives from cinnamic acid. So
the plant is used in the perfume industry, as well as to flavour
wines and liqueurs.

Hedge Bedstraw   *Galium mollugo*
Bedstraw family   *Rubiaceae*

Characters: 25-80 (100) cm: flowers May-September. One of
the most common species of the bedstraw family in our area.
A stout, perennial with ascending 4-angled stems (with no
downward directed prickles), and flat leaves, 2-8 mm broad,
which narrow abruptly to a point. Flowers with no distinct
tube, the lobes rounded, awned. Flower stalks rather longer
than the flowers. Fruit wrinkled.—**Habitat:** meadows,
grassland neither very dry nor very damp, pathsides, hedges,
copses, edges of woods; stony places. Up to heights of 2100
m.—**Distribution:** over most of Europe except the north. In
the British Isles, common in the south. As with many other
members of the family, Hedge Bedstraw contains a substance
in its roots which can be isolated and used as a natural (red)
dye.

Crosswort   *Cruciata laevipes*
Bedstraw family   *Rubiaceae*

Characters: 10-50 (70) cm; flowers April-May. Easily identifiable by the leaves, yellowish green, broadly ovate and roughly hairy, with 3 veins in whorls of 4. Stem hairy, weak, 4-angled. Flowers yelow to greenish yellow, 4-lobed, in whorled clusters, up the stem. Fruit smooth, black when ripe, on curved fruit stalks.—**Habitat:** weedy edges of hedges, fences and ditches; banks, copses; low-lying woods; up to 1600 m.—**Distribution:** West and Central Europe, and north Mediterranean area. Frequent in England, Wales and South Scotland. Very rare elsewhere. A plant that likes warmth and light or partial shade, with a creeping rootstock, mainly pollinated by flies and bees. A red dye can be extracted from the roots. The plant has also a certain importance medicinally.

Field Scabious   *Knautia arvensis*
Teasel family   *Dipsaceae*

Characters: 30-120 cm; flowers May-October. Perennial, with long-stalked, bluish mauve flower-heads. Corolla four lobed; the outer florets distinctly enlarged, rayed. Recepticle scaleless, unlike the genus *Scabiosa.* Involucre in two rows, its bracts hairy, ovate to lanceolate. Stem leaves, especially the middle ones, deeply pinnately-lobed, grey-green; the basal often entire. Stem short, hairy or bristly below.—**Distribution:** all over Europe and a large part of Asia, but chiefly in the west. Found in the British Isles, most common in the south.

Field Scabious, like other scabiouses, is often mistaken for a member of the *Compositae* (daisy family). The clearest point of recognition is the fact that the stamens of the teasel family are not fused, whereas those of the daisy family are generally united into a tube. Field Scabious is a deep-rooting plant. Pollination is by bees and lepidoptera (burnet moths). The seeds have nutritious appendage (elaisome), which ants eat, thus helping to disperse them.

Common Valerian   *Valeriana officinalis*
Valerian family   *Valerianaceae*

Characters: 50-150 cm; flower June-August. Sturdy perennial with deeply ridged, glossy, hairless, sometimes reddish stem, with 6-9 pairs of leaves, about 20 cm long, the upper sessile, the lower stalked, all with narrow lanceolate leaflets. Flowers bisexual, pale pink, with 3 stamens, slightly asymmetrical. As the fruit ripens a tuft of hair (pappus) pours out from the calyx; the fruit itself is longish ovoid, hairless, not over 5 mm long.—**Habitat:** (damp) edges of woods, copses, clearings in woods, grassy places, ditches and banks; in mountain areas up to about 2000 m.—**Distribution:** all over temperate Europe, and all over the British Isles. The habitats show that Common Valerian is a plant requiring light, or at least only partial shade. The characteristic valerian aroma arises from the production of essential oils and isovalerian acid, hence its great pharmaceutical importance. Because of the strong aroma, the underground parts of the plant were once used to bait rat traps. The other representative of the genus among our wild flowers is Marsh Valerian, *V. dioica,* with pinnate central and upper stem leaves, which is found in damp meadow land.

Field Bindweed   *Convolvulus arvensis*
Bindweed family   *Convolvulaceae*

Characters: 30-60 cm; flowers May-october. Perennial with a twining, partly prostrate stem, leaves spear or arrow-shaped, almost hairless. The solitary flowers, on long stalks, from the leaf axils, vary in volour from deep pink to white, generally there are 5 distinct mauve stripes. Flowers 15-25 mm long and up to 20 mm diameter; stigmas 2. Ovary and capsule 2 chambers. Calyx without bracteole.—**Habitat:** fields, gardens, rubbish dumps, roadsides, by fences; up to heights of 1200 m.—**Distribution:** all over the world in warm temperate climates. Common in South Britain, scarcer elsewhere. Field Bindweed is a pioneer plant among weeds. It can be considered an indicator of warmth because of its relatively great need for such conditions. Its liking for cultivated areas explains the fact that it has now spread almost all over the world. Pollination is by flies and bees.

Great Bindweed   *Calystegia sepium*
Bindweed family   *Convolvulaceae*

Characters: 100-300 cm; flowers June-September. Hairless, sturdy plant climbing with twining stems. Leaves more or less arrow-shaped, 5-15 cm long, flowers 3-6 cm large, white or pink. Stamens glandular-hairy below. The 2 large, heart-shaped, greenish bracteoles are flat, not inflated, and almost twice as long as the hairless calyx.—**Habitat:** gardens, hedges, fences, pathsides, banks, among reeds and sedges; up to 1200 m.—**Distribution:** Europe as far as Iceland; all over the temperate world. Often found in the British Isles, scarce in the North. The Great Bindweed, with its large underground stems, is an invasive pioneer plant. It is pollinated by moths, especially hawk-moths, and hover flies. Sea Bindweed, *Calystegia soldanella,* a prostrate plant with kidney-shaped, fleshy leaves and smaller pink flowers is found in coastal areas, mainly in Western and Southern Europe.

Viper's Bugloss *Echium vulgare*

Borage family *Boraginaceae*

Characters: 30-100 cm; flowers June-October. Flowers bell or funnel-shaped, slightly irregular, with a tendency to monosymmetry; first pink, then blue, longer than the calyx (about 15 mm). Stamens of different lengths, longer than the corolla. Stem leaves longish-lanceolate sessile, stiffly bristly, like the stout stem. The stalked rosette leaves indicate the biennial nature of the plant.—**Habitat:** among other weeds by pathsides and on railway embankments, in quarries, on rubbish dumps and sandy places. Prefers stony situations; in the Alps up to heights of 1300 m.—**Distribution:** throughout most of Europe, widespread in the British Isles. The plant's habitat and distribution indicate its ecological nature. It is one that likes warmth, whose roots go down as far as 2.5 m, a pioneer plant which can quickly colonize a vacant area. While the flowers of the borage family are generally radially symmetrical (several symmetrical axes) those of Viper's Bugloss have become monosymmetric (one symmetrical axis) to better adapt to pollination by insects. Viper's Bugloss can be regarded as a typical transitional form with this tendency. The closely related family of *Lamiaceae* (the Labiate family) shows a further development of this, having exclusively monosymmetrical flowers. The fruits are dispersed by the wind, or by attachment to animals etc. The plant was formerly regarded as of value medicinally.

Common Comfrey   *Symphytum officinale*

Borage family   *Boraginaceae*

Characters: 30-100 cm; flowers May-September. Flowers yellowish white or pinkish mauve, in a coil, an inflorescence typical of the family. A single branch overtops the main stem alternately left and right. The snail-like shape of the inflorescence is characteristic. Corolla 1.5 cm long, with very long scales in the tube. Leaves lanceolate, up to 25 cm long, running down on to the stem, which is erect, stout, and covered with stiff hairs.—**Habitat:** damp meadows, the banks of streams, ditches, low-lying woods, boggy ground; up to 1000 m.—**Distribution:** Europe and Asia. Widespread in the British Isles. A deep rooted plant, as far down as 1.80 m; likes light or partial shade, indicates a base of rich soil. Flies and bees pollinate the flowers, though some self-pollination also occurs. The single seeded fruit is dispersed by ants. The specific epithet *(officinale)* indicates the pharmaceutical attributes of the plant, whose roots are used to heal wounds The word derives from *officina*—a monastatic herb-store.

Narrow-leaved Lungwort

Pulmonaria (angustifolia)

Borage family   *Boraginaceae*

Characters: 15-30 cm; flowers March-May. Perennial; flowers red, turning to blue. Instead of scales, the corolla tube bears 5 tufts of hairs, longer than the calyx. Leaves of the basal, non-flowering shoots narrow lanceolate, narrowing very gradually below. Stem leaves unstalked, stem bristles with glandular hairs.—**Habitat:** deciduous woods, copses.—**Distribution:** East and Central Europe, not in Britain where the similar *P. longifolia* grows in Hants and Dorset. A plant which likes warmth and partial shade, pollinated mainly by bees and bumble bees. The single-seeded fruits, are dispersed by ants. The name indicates that Lungwort was formerly used as a medicinal herb.

Deadly Nightshade   *Atropa belladonna*

Nightshade family   *Solanaceae*

Characters: 50-150 cm; flowers June-August. A striking herbaceous plant with solitary-stalked, violet flowers, dirty yellow inside, from the leaf axils, corolla bell-shaped, 25-30 mm, with 5 short lobes. The calyx becomes slightly enlarged as the fruit, a shiny black globular juicy berry, ripens. It is often possible to see flowers, unripe fruits and ripe fruits on one plant at the same time. Leaves ovate, pointed, entire, harrowed into the stalk, up to 20 cm long.—**Habitat:** clearings in woods, deciduous and mixed woods, woodland paths, bomb sites; found up to heights of 1700 m on soil containing lime, porphyry or gneiss.—**Distribution:** Central and Southern Europe, absent from Scandinavia. Scattered on the British isles, chiefly in the South East. Deadly Nightshade has many ecological features. While the plant itself prefers light or partial shade, the seeds can germinate only in full light. The flowers are pollinated by bumblebees; the glossy berries are dispersed by birds, who are obviously immune to the dangerous poison. The berries and indeed the whole plant, contain the alkaloids atropine, hyoscamine and hyoscine, which in humans will cause enlargement of the pupils of the eyes and paralysis, usually leading to death. In small amounts, these substances are still used on a large scale medicinally as stimulants. Formerly the plant was even applied as a cosmetic for instance to whiten the skin, remove freckles, and indeed, enlarge the pupils by the effect of atropine! The scientific epithet refers to this: *belladonna* = beautiful woman.

Common Toadflax   *Linaria vulgaris*

Figwort family   *Scrophulariaceae*

Characters: 20-80 cm; flowers June-September. A striking, easily recognised plant, with numerous sulphur-yellow flowers in a long raceme. The lower lips have striking orange marks which serve as honey-guides to insects. Spur fairly straight; flowers without spur 16-22 mm long, with spur 22-30 mm long. Leaves alternate, close together, linear to lanceolate, blue-green. Seeds broad-winged in capsules more than twice as long as the calyx.—**Habitat:** sunny, open weedy areas; ditches by roads, paths and railways, rubbish dumps, quarries, fields, clearings; in the Alps up to heights of about 1100 m.—**Distribution:** all over Europe except the extreme north and south. Frequent in England, Wales, scattered Scotland and Ireland.

Common Toadflax exhibits a special form of vegetative propagation, as well as the normal sexual reproduction: it is a pioneer plant, colonizing waste ground, with roots going down 1 m which produce many new shoots. A dense underground mat is thus formed, which also helps consolidate the soil. Common Toadflax, which likes light and warmth, is pollinated by insects or by self-pollination; the winged seeds are dispersed by wind, but ants also help to spread them. The genus represents a clearly defined systematic grouping within the Figwort family. Its characeristics are the mono-symmetrical, spurred flowers, with only four stamens. The more primitive genus *Verbascum* (Mullein), on the other hand, has radially symmetrical flowers with 5 stamens. The genera *Antirrhinum* (Snapdragon), *Cymbalaria* (Ivy-leaved Toadflax), and *Scrophularia* (Figwort) also have mono-symmetrical flowers; in consequence we find a reduction in the number of stamens. For instance, the genus *Veronica* (Speedwell) has only two stamens.

Germander Speedwell   *Veronica chamaedrys*

Figwort family   *Scrophulariaceae*

Characters: 10-30 cm; flowers April-August. A good character is the presence of 2 lines of hairs on the stem. Leaves short stalked, flowers sky-blue in racemes, of only a few flowers, a stalk for the leaf axils. The flower, with its 4 sepals and only 2 stamens, shows considerable divergence from the original 5-partite form, as still seen in the Mullein, *Verbascum.* Capsule shorter than the calyx.—**Habitat:** by hedges and copses, meadows, banks, by paths, edges of woods, open dry woods; up to heights of 2200 m.—**Distribution:** all over Europe, mainly in the west. Common all over the British Isles.

Germander Speedwell is a plant which likes light or partial shade, but it will flower only in light and not in shady situations. The reason for this may be found in the higher rate of photosynthesis in full light. Bees and flies are the main pollinators; ants disperse the seeds. It is a member of the genus of the Figwort family and is the richest species in our area. In identifying them, the way the flowers are borne, the shape of the fruit capsule and the length of the fruit stalks are of particular importance, along with the amount of hair on the plant and the shape of the leaves. In the way the flowers are borne, we can divide them into 3 groups; in either lateral spikes or racemes (i.e. there are only leaves at the top of the stem), or in terminal spikes or racemes. The third group comprises species with flowers solitary on stalks in the leaf axils. Germander Speedwell belongs to the first group, as does the Heath Speedwell, *V. officinalis,* which has hairs fairly evenly distributed all over the stem — like various other species found in damp ground. Representatives of the second group, besides many Alpine species are Wall Speedwell, *V. arvensis,* Spring Speedwell, *V. verna,* and Fingered Speedwell, *V. triphyllos,* the last two very rare in Britain. The third group comprises mainly those found in fields, gardens, on rubbish dumps or waste ground, e.g. Common Field Speedwell, *V. persica,* Green Field Speedwell, *V. agrestis,* and Grey Field Speedwell, *V. polita.*

Eyebright *Euphrasia officinalis*
Figwort family *Scrophulariaceae*

Characters: 5-25 cm; flowers June-October. A very variable, group species. Flowers 5-15 mm long, white or mauvish sections and yellow spots. 4-toothed calyx, 4 stamens. Leaves toothed 2 cm., unstalked, longish ovate, sometimes glandular hairy, like the inflorescence. Stem covered with curly whitish hairs.—**Habitat:** dry grassland, meadows in mountain, heathy or marshy areas, sheep pastures; up to 2300 m.—**Distribution:** over most of Europe and all over the British Isles. Eyebright is a semi-parasite, which derives the energy to create organic material for its own use by photosynthesis, but also taps the roots of other plants to derive water and nutrient salts. It is still used as a medicinal herb for eye troubles. The microspecies illustrated is *Euphrasia rostkoviana* which occurs in the west of the British Isles.

Hoary Plantain *Plantago media*
Plantain family *Plantaginaceae* (Picture below left)

Characters: 15-50 cm; flowers May-September. Perennial, with broadly elliptic, short-stalked leaves, usually entire, 5-9 veined, with short, soft hairs on both sides. The cylindrical flower spike, 3-8 cm long, is noticeably shorter than the stem. Flowers silvery-white stamens, purple with mauve anthers. Fruit usually 4-seeded.—**Habitat:** meadows, roadsides, banks, dry grassland; up to 1800 m.—**Distribution:** Europe and Asia. In Britain common on alkaline soils; very rare elsewhere. Plantains are interesting from the point of view of floral ecology; the stamens and stigmas ripen at different times — the plants go first through a feminine and then a masculine stage. This arrangement which ensures cross-fertilization, is called protogyny.

Ribwort Plantain *Plantago lanceolata*
Plantain family *Plantaginaceae* (Picture below right)

Characters: 10-60 cm; flowers April-October. Leaves lanceolate with 3-7 distinct parallel veins, basal rosette with leaves about 15 cm long, narrowed below base. Flower spikes longish ovate, corolla, brownish, stamens white. Fruits with two sticky seeds, dispersed by clinging to animals etc.—**Habitat:** meadows, heaths, park turf, banks, pathsides, up to 1900 m.—**Distribution:** all over the world in cool to temperate climates. Abundant all over the British Isles.

Bugle   *Ajuga reptans*
Labiate family   *Lamiaceae* (Labiatae)

Characters: 15-50 cm; flowering season April-August. Plant with runners. Flowers blue, occasionally pink or white, in whorls at the top of the stem. Corolla tube with a ring of hairs inside. Upper lip very small, short and two-lobed; lower lip large, three-lobed. Leaves undivided, longish-ovate, entire or slightly toothed; rosette leaves long-stalked.—**Habitat:** meadows, banks, copses, woods; reaching heights of about 1700 m.—**Distribution:** deciduous wooded areas of West and Central Europe, the northern Mediterranean region; also native in Scandinavia. Frequent throughout the British Isles. Bugle is a plant which likes full light or partial shade, and is an indicator of base-rich soil. In addition to pollination by insects, self-pollination occurs. The species is spread by the dispersal of its seeds by ants and by its runners. Our other two rare species of bugle do not have runners. Very rarely hybrids occur.

Ground Ivy   *Glechoma hederacea*
Labiate family   *Lamiaceae* (Labiatae)

Characters: 15-60 cm; flowering season March-June. Perennial, with prostrate stems rooting at the nodes. Flowers violet-blue on short stalks in l-sided whorls of 2-3. Stamens and style longer than the corolla tube, calyx with 5 more or less equal teeth. Bracts deep purple. Leaves roundish to kidney-shaped. Somewhat glossy above, dull green to reddish beneath.—**Habitat:** meadows, hedges, roadsides, walls, low-lying woods, often beneath trees. Occuring up to 1400 m.—**Distribution:** all over Europe, parts of Asia; prefers coastal areas. Common throughout the British isles except the extreme North. Ground Ivy likes partial shade or full light, and is generally pollinated by insects. The fruits are dispersed by sticking to animals or by ants (myrmecochory, see Hepatica, p.18). The species is one of those formerly used medicinally for coughs and even worms.

Hemp-Nettle *Galeopsis pubescens*

Labiate family *Lamiaceae* (Labiatae) (Picture top left)

Characters: 20-60 cm; flowering season June-October. Annual, with flowers 18-25 mm long. Corolla tube, usually dark red, more than twice as long as the calyx with a yellow throat, and two conical projections at the base of the lower lip. The nodes of the stem are slightly swollen, more or less appressed hairy, with a few spreading bristles and long-stalked glands.—**Habitat:** edges of paths and fields, copses, clearings in woods—base rich, loam and clay; up to 1600 m.—**Distribution:** over much of Europe, but unknown in the British Isles, where however, similar species occur.

Large-Flowered Hemp Nettle

Galeopsis speciosa

Labiate family *Lamiaceae* (Labiatae) (Picture top right)

Characters: 30-100 cm; flowering June-October. Easily identified by the large (20-45 mm) yellow flowers, with a purple central lobe on the lower lip. Corolla tube about twice as long as the calys. Stem covered with stiff, bristly hairs below the nodes.—**Habitat:** woods, clearings, hedges, path-sides, banks, weedy areas; growing up to heights of 1900 m.—**Distribution:** many parts of Europe; mainly concentrated in the East. In the British Isles scattered in arable land. Not infrequent in the North.

Self-Heal *Prunella vulgaris*

Labiate family *Lamiaceae* (labiatae)

Characters: 5-30 cm; flowering June-September. Perennial with violet flowers, 7-15 mm long, and purple bracts. Calyx irregular 2-lipped, corolla tube straight. Leaves 15-30 mm, longish ovate, slightly hairy, stalked. Stems erect or ascending, slightly hairy. The plant has short runners.—**Habitat:** grassy areas, e.g. parks, pasture land, woodland paths, banks; in the Alps up to 2200 m.—**Distribution:** mainly in North and Central Europe and Asia, but occurs all over the temperate world. Common throughout the British Isles.

Self-heal uses the same mechanism for dispersing its seeds as Field Pennycress; they are flung out when the fruit is struck by falling raindrops (see p.62 above).

Yellow Archangel   *Lamiatrum gelteobdolon*

Labiate family   *Lamiaceae* (Labiatae)   (Picture top left)

Characters: 30-60 cm; flowering April-July. Perennial, with golden yellow flowers. Lower lip with three pointed lobes, and reddish or brownish markings. Corolla-tube 20 mm long, hairy on the outside. Leaves stalked, heart-shaped to ovate, serrate, sparsely hairy. The sterile shoots form runners.— **Habitat:** shady woods, copses, low-lying woods.—**Distribution:** Over most of Europe. Frequent over most of the British Isles. Bees are the main pollinators of this plant.

Spotted Dead-Nettle   *Lamium maculatum*

Labiate family   *Lamiaceae* (labiatae)   (Picture top right)

Characters: 20-80 cm; flowering April-November. A perennial with purple flowers, 20-30 mm long, with dark markings on the lower lip and a curved corolla tube with a purple ring of erect hairs. Lower leaves up to 8 cm long, very long-stalked (4 cm).—**Habitat:** woods, especially the edges of woods, hedges, ditches by roadsides, weedy margins of shady places. Up to heights of 2000 m.—**Distribution:** continental areas of Europe and Asia, but not in Northern Europe. In Britain, a rare survivor from gardens, nearly always with white blotches on the leaves. Spotted Dead-nettle likes partial shade, and is a creeping pioneer plant. It is pollinated by insects; as with other Dead-nettles, the seeds are dispersed by ants.

Read Dead-Nettle   *Lamium purpureum*

Labiate family   *Lamiaceae* (Labiatae)

Characters: 10-30 cm; flowering March-November. Bracts ovate-triangular, irregularly notched, stalked and, like the leaves, often tinged red. Flowers in close whorls, purplish red, 10-15 mm, twice as long as the calyx, corolla tube with transversing of hairs inside. The plant has an unpleasant smell.—**Habitat:** A weed of fields or gardens, or rubbish dumps, by paths, supremely a ruderal plant; up to heights of 1800 m.—**Distribution:** Europe and Asia, especially in the north and centre. Common over most of the British Isles. Read Dead-nettle has been a weed of cultivation since the Bronze Age; it is a typical indicator of nitrogen in the soil, a plant that likes light, and one of the few winter-flowering plants in our wild flora.

White Dead-Nettle *Lamium album*
Labiate family *Lamiaceae* (labiatae)

Characters: 20-60 cm; flowering April-October. A familiar wild plant, perennial, with large (20-25 mm) white flowers. Corolla with an oblique ring of hairs inside, longer than the calyx, curved; upper lip with long hairs. Leaves long and pointed, sharply serrate, stalked, 3-7 cm long. The plant forms creeping rhizomes.—**Habitat:** roadsides, fences, walls, ditches, hedges, near cattle sheds, rubbish dumps. A typical ruderal plant. Up to heights of 1800 m in the Alps.—**Distribution:** Europe and Asia. Common over most of Britain, local in the North of Scotland and in Ireland.
White Dead-nettle is a creeping pioneer plant through its rhizomes. Like Red Dead-nettle, it is an indicator of nitrogen. A light-loving plant, it is principally pollinated by bumble bees, but self-pollination also occurs. The flowers are used for medicinal purposes.

Hedge Woundwort *Stachys silvatica*
Labiate family *Lamiaceae* (labiatae) (Picture below right)

Characters: 30-100 cm; flowers June-September. Flowers deep purplish red, occasionally pink, twice as long as the calyx, in leafless whorls of 4-10. Leaves heart-shaped to ovate, pointed, serrate; the lower especially are long-stalked; general appearance nettle-like. Stem erect, glandular hairy above, the whole plant rough-haired. When rubbed it gives off an unpleasant smell.—**Habitat:** damp, mixed deciduous woods, copses, low-lying woodland, on banks, beside woodland paths; up to heights of 1700 m.—**Distribution:** all over Europe except for Iceland. Common all over the British Isles. The plant is typical of those that will germinate in dark places, preferring shade or partial shade.

Marsh Woundwort *Stachys palustris*
Labiate family *Lamiaceae* (Labiatae) (Picture below left)

Characters: 30-100 cm; flowering June-September. Corolla light purple, twice as long as the calyx. Flowers in whorls of 4-11, in a nearly leafless inflorescence. Leaves longish lanceolate with a few sparsely, appressed hairs, or almost hairless; upper leaves sessile, lower stalked.—**Habitat:** ditches banks, damp fields, marshes; damp clay and loam soil; up to 1200 m.—**Distribution:** All over Europe except for Iceland. Frequent in the British Isles. It very much needs full light.

Meadow Clary   *Salvia pratensis*

Labiate family   *Lamiaceae* (Labiatae)

Characters: 30-60 (80) cm; flowers April-August. Perennial with violet blue, occasionally pink or white flowers, which are 20-25 mm long, about three times as long as the rather irregularly toothed calyx. Inflorescence glandular hairy. Bracts green, deflexed, shorter than the calyx. Leaves irregularly scalloped, rather wrinkled, mostly radical and stalked, the upper sessile.—**Habitat:** dry, sunny places; roadsides, banks, slopes, grassy places, especially on chalk; up to 1600 m.—**Distribution:** in temperate Continental areas, from the north Mediterranean through Central Europe to Scandinavia (naturalized in Northern Europe). It is rather rare in England; in the south only. Meadow Clary, a plant which likes warmth and light, with roots going down over 1 m, is a showy meadow flower. Its seeds are dispersed by sticking to animals. A particularly interesting feature is its method of pollination; the mechanism employed was described by Christian Konrad Sprengel (1750-1816), one of the founders of the science of floral ecology. The male organs of the flowers mature first (protandry); they have only two stamens, which are converted into a levering device. Only half the front of the stamen is fertile, the longer arm of the lever; the shorter arm at the back broadens out and forms a flat plate in conjunction with the corresponding arm of the other stamen. Bumble bees visiting the flower must press against this plate in order to reach the nectar. The levering mechanism causes the longer arm to descend, brushing pollen on to the insect's back. The pollen is then transferred to the stigmas of older, female, flowers, which have by this time risen to the same height. This ensures cross-fertilization.

Large Thyme *Thymus pulegioides*
Labiate family *Lamiaceae* (Labiatae)

Characters: 5-15 cm; flowers June-October. The most important character is the sharply squared stem, which has rows of hairs at the 4 corners. Flowers pinkish purple in fairly loosely arranged whorls. At least the upper calyx teeth have hairs at the edges (ciliate). Leaves hairless, or with a few hairs on the upper surface, scarcely increasing in size from bottom to top. Stem erect. Plant without runners, aromatic.—**Habitat:** dry meadow land, heaths, edges of woods and paths, slopes, ant heaps, gravel pits, rocky ground, sandhills; up to 2300 m.—**Distribution:** almost all over Europe; very common in West and Central Europe and Asia. Quite common on the alkaline soils of South Britain, rare elsewhere. A plant which likes warmth and light, with roots down to 1 m; a creeping pioneer, and an indicator of poor soil. Its colonization of ant heaps can be explained by the dispersal of its seeds by ants. The practical uses of this plant extend from its importance to beekeepers (bees visit it for nectar and pollinate it) to its medicinal uses, which derive from its essential oils, especially thymol. Its use in cough mixtures is well-known. Common Thyme, *T. vulgaris,* however, native in Southern Europe, is of greater practical importance.

Marjoram *Origanum vulgare*
Labiate family *Lamiaceae* (Labiatae)

Characters: 30-60 cm; flowers July-September. Aromatic perennial, with terminal or lateral inflorescences. Corolla pink; upper lip erect, the lower 3-lobed. Corolla tube longer than the calyx. Bracts and calyx teeth generally more or less tinged with purple. Leaves 15-45 mm long, ovate, entire or slightly toothed, stalked. Plant usually rather hairy.—**Habitat:** dry grassland, open scrub, edges of woods, hedges, slopes; in hilly areas growing up to heights of over 1800 m.—**Distribution:** All over Europe except for Iceland; in large parts of Western Asia. Now widespread in North America. Widely distributed in the British Isles, chiefly on alkaline soils. The species is of practical use as a source of nectar for bees, but also as a medicinal and culinary herb. A sub-species, Sweet Marjoram, is well-known.

Harebell   *Campanual rotundifolia*
Bellflower family   *Campanulaceae*

Characters: 10-50 cm; flowers June-September. A perennial with many flowers in loose panicles. Flower buds erect stalked, starting to nod just before the flower opens; flowers 10-20 mm long, light blue; the outer third of the corolla is split into ovate lobes. Calyx teeth awl-shaped. Stem leaves narrowly linear, generally hairless. For precise identification, the roundish, heart or kidney shaped lower leaves are important, but they have generally withered by the time the plant flowers. Stem finely pubescent below.—**Habitat:** poor grassland, heaths, grassy places, meadows, roadsides, dry woods, among rocks, sandhills; growing even as high as 2500 m.—**Distribution:** All over Europe, except for Portugal and Turkey. Generally one could say the distribution was circumpolar, with the main concentration in north Europe and Asia. Common over most of the British Isles. Rare in South and East Ireland.

Harebell has a creeping root stock and puts down roots as far as 1.20 m. From its habitats, it can be seen that it is an indicator of poor soil and a light-loving plant. Pollination is mainly by bees. Here a mechanism typical of the Harebell comes into play, one which would normally prevent self-pollination: the phenomenon called protandry, in which the male organs of the flower mature first. The stamens ripen, the insects in search of nectar take on a load of ripe pollen, and carry it to flowers which have reached a more advanced, female, stage of development. The ripening at different times of male and female flowers organs, in conjunction with pollination by insects, ensures cross-fertilization, and thus a new combination of inherited characters. This again generally results in the production of more fruit and better adaptation to local (or changed) environmental conditions. Protogyny (maturation of the female organs first), which does not often occur in flowering plants, has the same effect (for instance in the genus Plantago, see p. 98 above).

Spiked Rampion   *Phyteuma spicatum*

Bellflower family   *Campanulaceae*

Characters: 20-80 cm; flowers May-July. An unbranched perennial, inflorescence ovate at first, later spike-like. When ripe the spike may reach a length of 12 cm. Flowers yellowish white, corolla lobes joined at the top. Lower leaves long-stalked, heart-shaped, double-scalloped or serrate, the upper unstalked, linear-lanceolate.—**Habitat:** especially in deciduous woods, but also found in mixed coniferous woods; mountain pastures up to heights of 2100 m.—**Distribution:** Over most of Europe, naturalised in Scandinavia. In Britain known only from one small area in Sussex. Pollination by insects and dispersal by wind are necessary for the spread of this plant, which was formerly collected from the wilds to eat as a wild vegetable. A related species is Round-headed Rampion, *Phyteuma tenerum,* (local on chalk in the South of England). Most species of *Phyteuma* have blue to deep violet flowers in globular flowerheads or in ovate to cylindrical spikes. The majority in Europe are confined to the Alps, only a few being found lower down.

Yarrow   *Achillea Millefolium*
Daisy family   *Asteraceae* (Compositae)

Characters: 15-80 cm; flowers May-October. A stout perennial, with flower-heads in dense clusters. The disc and ray florets white, sometimes pink or reddish. Involucral bracts long with dark brown margins. Leaves alternate, regularly 2-pinnate with short, linear, pointed segments. Stem erect, leafy.—**Habitat:** meadows, pasture land, grassy places, grassland not too wet or too dry, edges of fields and paths, cultivated land; up to about 1900 m in the Alps.—**Distribution:** almost cosmopolitan; the whole of Europe; the whole of the British Isles.

Yarrow, with its creeping rootstock, is a pioneer plant. It has a certain importance as a consolidator of the soil, and an indicator of the presence of nutrients and as a fodder plant. Its main practical use is medicinal, for infusions of yarrow tea.

Pineapple Weed   *Matricaria matricarioides*
Daisy family   *Asteraceae* (Compositae)   (Picture below left)

Characters: 5-40 cm; flowers May-August. Annual, with strong chamomile scent; distinguishing features are the greenish yellow, conical flower-heads, which lack ray florets. Disc florets, 4-lobed. Involucral bracts longish, hairless, with a broad, transparent margin. Leaves 2 to 3-pinnate, with narrowly linear, pointed segments. Fruit 4-ribbed, sticky (dispersed by adhering to animals).—**Habitat:** waste ground, rubbish dumps, grassy areas near human settlements; up to 1000 m.—**Distribution:** Widespread in central and North Europe, world-wide in cool to temperate areas. Common throughout the British Isles. A species which has fairly recently become naturalized in Europe, its original home being North-East Asia (and possibly North America). Like other species of chamomile, it is used medicinally.

Scentless Chamomile   *Matricaria inodora*
Daisy family   *Asteraceae* (Compositae)   (Picture below right)

Characters: 25-80 cm; flowers June-November. Receptacle hemispherical, solid. Ray florets 12-20, white; disc florets yellow. Almost scentless. Tips of leaves furrowed beneath.—**Habitat:** Among other weeds, on rubbish dumps, roadsides, fields; in the foothills; up to 1300 m.—**Distribution:** temperate continental areas. Widely introduced, probably originated in Western Asia. Common throughout most of the British Isles.

Daisy   *Bellis perennis*

Daisy family   *Asteraceae* (Compositae)

Characters: 3-20 cm; flowers February-November. Perennial rosette plant with solitary flower-heads on leafless stems. Ray florets white, disc florets yellow. Involucral bracts bluntly lanceolate. Fruit with no pappus (tufts of hair on the achenes). Leaves spatulate to obovate, narrowed below.—**Habitat:** pastures, meadows, grassland, roadsides; in the Alps up to heights of 1860 m.—**Distribution:** all over Europe, all over the British Isles. Daisies like warmth and light. Insects pollinate the plants; the fruits are shaken out by the wind. This type of dispersal by wind is known as *anemochory.*

Ox-Eye Daisy   *Leucanthemum vulgare*

Daisy family   *Asteraceae* (Compisitae)

Characters: 20-80 cm; flowers May-September. A characteristic meadow flower with white ray florets and yellow disc florets (no pappus, see Daisy above). Flowerheads solitary, long-stalked. Involucral bracts green, longish lanceolate with brownish, transparent margins. Upper stem leaves shorter than the inter-nodes, undivided, spathulate, scalloped or serrate and semi-amplexical, the basal stalked.—**Habitat:** meadows, grassy places, roadsides, sunny slopes, rocky places, reaching heights of over 2300m.—**Distribution:** all over Europe, mainly in the west; all over the British isles. Ox-Eye Daisy, also known as Marguerite and Moon Daisy, is a deep-rooting plant, colonizing waste ground. It is pollinated mainly by insects (flies, beetles and moths), but self-pollination also occurs. The fruits are dispersed by the wind or by herbivores.

Groundsel   *Senecio vulgaris*
Daisy family   *Asteraceae* (Compositae)

Characters: 10-30 cm; flowers February-November. The outer involucre consists of 8-12 short bracts, black at the tips. There are 21 inner bracts. Fruit about 2 mm long, with downy hairs along the ribs and a long white pappus. Stem leaves pinnately divided and lobed, generally auricled (with an ear-shaped base embracing the stem) and usually hairless.—**Habitat:** open weedy areas, fields, gardens, rubbish dumps, paths, walls, clearings; up to heights of 1900 m.—**Distribution:** all over Europe; all over the temperate world; all over the British Isles. This annual has a long history as a weed of cultivation; a light-loving plant which requires moisture for its development. it is one of our few winter-flowering plants. In the normal way self-pollination occurs, and the fruits are dispersed by the wind or stick to animals. Groundsel used to be considered a medicinal herb. Today its alkaloid content warns us that it may be poisonous.

Coltsfoot   *Tussilage farfara*
Daisy family   *Asteraceae* (Compositae)

Characters: 5-20 (30) cm; flowers February-April. The flower-stems, terminating in a solitary flower-head, have only scale leaves; the leaves proper (large, heart-shaped, covered with grey down on the under-sides) do not appear until the plant has flowered. Ray-florets narrow, yellow, in several rows. Fruit with a long, silky pappus.—**Habitat:** rubbish dumps, roadsides, railway embankments, gravel pits, damp fields, banks, stony meadows; growing at heights of up to 2300 m.—**Distribution:** North and Central Europe and Asia, and the north Mediterranean region; often introduced elsewhere, All over the British Isles. Coltsfoot is much valued medicinally, as a cough cure. An early-flowering plant, pollinated by bees and flies; the fruits dispersed by the wind. The seeds can germinate only in good light, and are controlled by a special pigmentation (phytochrome system).

Butterbur   *Petasites hybridus*
Daisy family   *Asteraceae* (Compositae)

Characters: 30-100 cm; flowers March-May. A striking, stout perennial, flowering stem appearing before the leaves; its large, ovate inflorescence consists of numerous densely packed, mauve-pink flower-heads, which in their turn are composed of many florets. Male flower-heads 7-12 mm long, about twice as long as the female which, however, have longer stalks. Bracts reddish, hairless, blunt. A marked feature is the enormous size of the basal leaves, up to 1 m long and 0.6 m broad, on long stalks with a deep furrow above, toothed, heart-shaped with rounded lobes, green and downy above; grey and furry beneath when young.—**Habitat:** water meadows, the banks of cool, rather fast-flowing water, damp woods and ravines; up to 1500 m.—**Distribution:** all over Europe, not originally a native of the North, but now naturalized there. All over the British Isles.

Its long, creeping rhizome enables Butterbur to colonize large areas quickly. It is thus a creeping pioneer plant, and is of importance in the consolidation of alluvial land. It has no particular light preferences but it does require a high degree of humidity if it is to grow well. Butterbur is usually one of the first plants in its habitats to flower. It is pollinated by bees. The cylindrical, hairy fruits are dispersed by the wind. It used formerly to be used medicinally.

Cabbage Thistle   *Cirsium oleraceum*
Daisy family   (Compositae)

Characters: 50-150 cm; flowers June-September. Stout, erect perennial with yellowish-white flower-heads, in clusters at the top of the stem, surrounded by slightly prickly involucral bracts. The amplexical stem leaves are edged with bristles, like the bracts, but are otherwise almost hairless. Lower leaves lanceolate, usually pinnately lobed. As with all thistles of the *Crisium* genusm the fruits have a feathery pappus; those of the closely related *Carduus* have an undivided pappus.—**Habitat:** damp meadows, marshes, banks, ditches, low-lying woods; up to heights of about 2000 m.—**Distribution:** the entire continental area of Europe and Asia; very rarely to be seen naturalized in the British Isles. Cabbage Thistle is a deep-rooting plant, liking full light or partial shade. Its flowers are pollinated by bees and butterflies; its fruits dispersed by the wind. In many areas it is used as a vegetable, hence the epithet and the English name.

Creeping Thistle   *Cirsium arvense*
Daisy family   (Compositae)

Characters: 50-120 cm; flowers July-September. The densely leafy branched stems bear many flower-heads, but non-flowering shoots often occur. The dull lilac flower-heads are composed of florets 5-cleft to the base (usually unisexual), and about 2-3 cm long. The hairy tuft (pappus) of the fruit eventually attains a length of 20-30 mm. Leaves deeply lobed to undivided, undulate, edged with spines, grey-green beneath, hardly cottony.—**Habitat:** Among weeds on rubbish dumps, in fields, clearings, on banks and beside paths. In the Alps up to heights of 2000 m.—**Distribution:** all over Europe and the British Isles; introduced widely in the northern hemisphere. On account of its creeping rootstock, Creeping Thistle is called a pioneer plant, with roots going down as far as 3 m. It is an indicator of the presence of nitrogen, and of loamy soil; it is one of man's oldest weeds of cultivation and particularly troublesome in arable fields. The fruits are widely dispersed by the wind.

Spear Thistle   *Cirsium vulgare*

Daisy family   *Astericae* (Compositae)

Characteristics: 60-150 (200) cm; flowers July-September. Flower-heads, purple to reddish-mauve, 2-4 cm broad, but distinctly longer; either solitary or in groups of 2-3. An important character is the decurrent leaves, usually covered underneath in grey down, whose pinnate segments are deeply toothed and prickly, ending in a long yellow spine.—**Habitat:** among weeds by roadsides, on banks, rubbish dumps, in clearings of woods. In hills, up to heights of about 1400 m.—**Distribution:** all over Europe; most common in West Europe, although it also occurs in Asia. It is common all over the British Isles. Spear Thistle occurs chiefly on loamy soil, and is an indicator of nitrates. It is a typical light-loving plant, usually pollinated by beetles and bumble bees. However, self-pollination is quite normal. The feathery pappus allows the wind to disperse the fruits effectively. There are about 15 species of *Crisium* in Central Europe, of which about 9 occur in Britain and about 60 in Europe generally. it is often difficult to identify a species precisely, since many hybridize. As well as the Creeping Thistle, *Crisum arvense,* and the Cabbage Thistle, mention should be made of a few other important species. Spiny Thistle found in the Alps, is identified by its whitish flower-heads and deeply pinnate-lobed leaves with their hard spines. Woolly Thistle, local on alkaline soils in England and Wales, is very like the species described above, but has non-decurrent leaves and spiny involucral bracts covered with cobwebby wool. Another similarly distributed species is Dwarf Thistle, *C. accaule.* Marsh Thistle, *C. palustre,* common in the British Isles, prefers marshy conditions, as does Melancholy Thistle, *C. heterophyllum,* of the North of Britain.

Brown Knapweed   *Centauria jacea*

Daisy family   *Asteraceae* (Compositae)

Characters: 20-80 cm; flowers June-October. An extremely variable plant, with purplish red flower-heads about 2 cm long. The ray-like outer florets are distinctly enlarged. The involuted bracts and their appendages are very important in naming knapweeds. In this case the appendages entirely conceal the bracts; they are dark to pale brown, the margins either entire or divided into narrow segments (lanciate). The fruit is hairy but has no pappus. Stem leaves unstalked, lanciate, undivided, the basal stalked and lobed.—**Habitat:** dry meadows, pastures, poor grassland, roadsides, copses; up to heights of 1900 m.—**Distribution:** Europe and Asia, mainly in the centre and South-east. Very rare in Britain, but the closely related *C. nigra* is abundant. Some interesting movements of the stamens can be observed in Brown Knapweed. Internal pressure (Turgor) of the cells in the stamens makes them curve outwards. Touching them causes a swift elastic contraction, so that the fused anthers are drawn downwards and the centrally placed style squeezes the pollen out of the anther tubes, bringing it into contact with the bodies of pollinating insects (especially bees). After an interval, the stamens resume their normal position, and are ready to be stimulated again.

Greater Knapweed   *Centaurea scabiosa*

Daisy family   *Asteraceae* (Compositae)

Characters: 30-120 cm; flowers June-September. The purplish-red flower-heads, over 2 cm in size, are long-stalked, and generally have enlarged outer florets. The involucral bracts are divided above the appendages and not clearly distinct from them. Leaves dark green, all pinnately lobed, the tips longish lanceolate. The plant is very variable.—**Habitat:** sunny grassland on poor soil, pastures, banks, roadsides, edges of copses, open woods. Prefers lime. Height up to 2100 m.—**Distribution:** Europe and Asia, but especially West and Central Europe. Frequent in England and Wales, local elsewhere. Greater Knapweed likes light or partial shade. Pollination is by bees and flies, the fruits dispersed by the wind and by ants.

Chicory   *Cichorium intybus*
Daisy family   *Asteraceae* (Compositae)

Characters: 25-120 cm; flowering July-September. A distinctive perennial with large (3-4 cm) flower-heads, which consist entirely of ray florets. Flower-heads mostly sessile with green glandular-hairy involucral bracts, the outer spreading and about half as long as the appressed inner. Pappus scale-like. Basal leaves deeply pinnate, bristly hairy beneath, stem leaves long lanceolate, entire or only slightly toothed. Stem stiffly erect with short branches, short bristly-hair.—**Habitat:** Pathsides, rubbish heaps, arable fields, pastures, reaching 1000 m.—**Distribution:** all over Europe, especially in the west, widely distributed in temperate climates elsewhere. It is local in the British Isles. Chicory is a typical companion of man. It is a deep-rooting pioneer plant, needing plenty of light for its optimal development. The flowers are generally open from 6 to 11 am. During this time they are pollinated by hover flies and bees. The fruits are spread by wind and by adhering to animals. Chicory has been known from ancient times as a medical and edible herb. The dried roots produce the coffee substitute (Chicory) and the leaves are used in salads. This latter use however is commoner in the related species *C. endivia,* which is cultivated for salads.

Smooth Sow-Thistle   *Sonchus oleraceus*

Daisy family   *Asteracea* (Compositae)

Characters: 30-100 cm; flowers June-October. Annual, generally with a branched stem. Flower-heads pale yellow, 20-25 mm, involucral bract 10-15 mm, hairless, eglandular. Fruit transversely wrinkled, 3 ribbed on each side. Stem-leaves soft, not glossy, generally pinnately lobed with smooth bristles at the margins. Auricles at the base of the leaves arrow-shaped, spreading, (an important identification feature).––**Habitat:** weedy areas beside paths, walls, on rubbish dumps, in gardens and fields; up to heights of about 1500 m in hilly country.—**Distribution:** almost all over Europe and the British Isles, has now spread all over the world in temperate zones. Smooth Sow-Thistle has long been a weed of cultivation, which helps to explain its wide distribution. As regards ecological factors, the plant needs light and warmth. It is a characteristic pioneer plant, and its roots, which go more than 1 m down, make it particularly persistent. Pollination is by insects (especially bees and hover-flies); it was formerly eaten in many areas as a salad. Another species of Sow-Thistle in our area is Prickly Sow-Thistle, *Sonchus asper,* which is the most similar to the Smooth Sow-Thistle, and equally common in the British Isles. The auricles of the stem leaves, however, are rounded and appressed, and the glossy leaves have distinct spines. The following two species have thick glandular hairs on the involucres and stems: Marsh Sow-Thistle, *S. palustris,* rare in England, with stem leaves narrowed below to an arrow-shaped base, blackish glandular hairs, while they are yellow on the Perennial Sow-Thistle. (See p.134 for a more detailed description).

Perennial Sow-Thistle   *Sonchus arvensis*
Daisy family   *Asteraceae* (Compositae)

Characters: 50-150 cm; flowers July-October. The stem of this species does not branch until it reaches the inflorescence. The golden-yellow flower-heads, 4-5 cm in size, are in loose clusters. The involucres and stems are dense with yellow glandular hairs. Style yellow (that of the Smooth Sow-thistle, see p. 132 above, is olive-brown), stem leaves glossy green, rounded, heart-shaped below, deeply divided into triangular lobes; upper leaves with rounded, appressed auricles. Fruit dark brown with 5 ribs running lengthwise on each side.—**Habitat:** fields, waste ground, rubbish dumps, banks, sandhills, salt-marshes; in mountains, up to 1700 m.—**Distribution:** most of Europe, except for Portugal, throughout the British Isles, now found all over the temperate world. The plant's tolerance of salt is worth noting. The leaves orient their position vertically, roughly north and south, in strong sunlight. The flowers open only in the morning, and are pollinated by bees, butterflies and moths.

Dandelions   *Taraxacum officinale*
Daisy family   *Asteraceae* (Compositae)

Characters: 10-50 cm; flowers April-October. Plant with all its leaves in a rosette, leaves coarsely serrate or toothed, to almost undivided; extremely variable. Stem hollow, hairless, pale, containing milky sap. Flower-heads large, yellow, with involucral bracts always reflexed; pappus of simple white hairs.—**Habitat:** pasture-land, meadows, fields, weedy areas, roadsides; in the mountains up to 2800 m.—**Distribution:** a Northern European and Asiatic species, but nowadays occurring all over the world. Abundant all over the British Isles. As a pioneer plant with a tap root going down as far as 2 m. a Dandelion can form embryos in its ovules without being fertilized; sexual propagation being replaced by asexual. Its dependence on ecological factors is shown particularly where light is concerned; the flower-heads will open only in the sun. Dandelions form part of the spring aspect (see above, p.66) of our meadows; they are a source of nectar for bees, and the young leaves can be used as a salad; they also have medicinal uses.

Meadow Saffron *Colchicum autumnale*
Lily family *Liliaceae*

Characters: 5-20 cm; flowers August-November. An interesting plant with an abnormal life cycle. Its solitary, pale mauve flowers appear in autumn. Their segments are elongated, and fused into a tube up to 20 cm long; styles 3, also up to 20 cm long. At the time of flowering there are no leaves; these come up in the spring, along with the fruit capsules. Leaves broadly lanceolate, glossy green, 15-20 cm long, usually in clusters of 3, and partly enclosing the capsule. The corm (bulb-like base of stem) up to 7 cm long, stores nutrients.—**Habitat:** damp meadows, low-lying woods; up to heights of 2000,.—**Distribution:** Meadow Saffron is most common in West and Central Europe, as well as in the North Mediterranean area. It is generally scarce in England and Wales and rare elsewhere. 3 of the many special features of this flower are: a) Because of the extreme length of the style, which has to be penetrated by the pollen tube since the ovary is underground, there is a relatively long time between pollination and fertilization. The pollen grains have to be nourished by the tissues of the style in order to survive at all. b) Every autumn a new corm is formed beside the old one, and the young flower shoot grows from this new corm. c) The name *Colchicum* comes from Colchis, the name given in antiquity to the coastal area of the east of the Black Sea, which features in Greek mythology as the home of poisons and enchantresses. The corm of the Meadow Saffron contains the very poisonous alkaloid, colchicine, which is synthesised from the amino-acids *phenylalanine* and *tyrosine.* Colchicine is used medicinally for the treatment of gout and rheumatism. Plant breeders use it to produce polypoloid plants (cells with many sets of chromosomes), since the effect of colchicine is to inhibit the separation of the chromosomes — the cells cease to divide.

May Lilly   *Maianthemum bifolium*
Lily family   *Liliaceae*

Characters: 5-15 cm; flowers April-June. Perennial with small, pure-white, 4-lobed flowers in terminal racemes. Unlike the Lily of the Valley, the flower stem is leafy (two short-stalked heart-shaped leaves); non-flowering specimens have only one leaf. The long, creeping underground rootstocks (rhizomes) are characteristic. Fruit bright red, globular (6 mm) berry.—**Habitat:** shady deciduous and coniferous woods, with plenty of humus in the soil, especially on acid soils.—**Distribution:** almost all over Europe, but very rare in England and probably introduced. The fact that the species is not found in the Iberian peninsula, Iceland and Ireland, the Southern Balkans and Asia Minor shows that the distribution is principally over the northern part of the continent. It is indeed among those with a circumpolar distribution. May Lily likes shady situations; as the list of habitats shows, it is an indicator of acid soil. The flowers are pollinated by insects, the fruits dispersed by various animals.

Lilly of the Valley   *Convallaria majalis*
Lily family   *Liliaceae*

Characters: 12-20 cm; flowers May-June. Perennial with flowers, one-sided racemes. The leafless stalk grows from a sheath of 2-3 elliptical, long-stemmed leaves. Perianth broadly bell-shaped, 5-8 mm long, white, with 6 short reflexed lobes. Flowers scented characteristically. Fruits, red berries.—**Habitat:** light deciduous woods (oak and beech woods), copses, likes chalk, found up to 1900 m.—**Distribution:** Europe and Asia, mainly in the West and central deciduous-wooded areas of Europe. Widespread in Britian, but never common. A plant which likes warmth and partial shade; mainly pollinated by insects, though self-pollination helps towards the formation of the fruit in many cases. The berries are dispersed by animals. Lily of the Valley is one of the poisonous species of the family, containing glycoside, which is used in the treatment of heart disease in a similar way to the digitalin produced from Foxgloves, *Digitalis purpurea*.

Common Solomon's Seal   *Polygonatum multiflorum*

Lily family   *Liliaceae*

Characters: 30-60 cm; flowers April-June. Perennial with an arching stem and a l-sided inflorescence. Flowers in groups of 2-5 in the axils of the bracts, perianth tubular bell-shaped, 6-lobed, white with green border. Stamens hairy. leaves alternate, in two rows up the stem, broadish, ovate, 5-12 cm long. The round stem is an important distinguished feature.—**Habitat:** shady places in copses and deciduous woods, likes lime, grows at heights of up to 1800 m.—**Distribution:** Europe and Asia, especially in central and southern wooded areas. Widespread in Britian.

Common Solomon's Seal, a typical shade-loving plant, is mainly pollinated by bumble bees, and its blue-black berries dispersed by animals. A special feature is the creeping underground stem (rhizome). Every year the terminal bud appears as an aerial shoot, while a lateral bud continues underground. The withered shoots of the previous years leave scars shaped like circular seals on the rhizome; hence the popular name. The plant is poisonous; it is still used medicinally, its rhizomes especially, in the treatment of inflammations and corns. Related species found in our area are the Angular Solomon's Seal, *Polygonatum oduratum,* with flowers singly or in pairs and an angular stem, very local on lime in England, and Whorled Solomon's Seal, *P. verticillatum,* with narrow leaves in whorls of 3-6, greenish white flowers in groups of 1-4 in the axils, and red berries. It is very rare — found in Scotland only.

INDEX

English Names

Latin Names